Cover: "A Gathering of Old Colored Men" - Chet Taylor
Design: Michael Godeck

First Edition 2019
©Lilly Taylor
chiringapress@gmail.com

ISBN 978-1-61012-043-2

Worlds Without End

Chet Taylor

Chiringa Press
Seguin, Texas 2019

Foreword

I fell in love with Chet Taylor years ago one evening in group therapy when he helped a woman in great emotional pain. He articulated his thoughts with insight and kindness, and knew how to direct everyone's attention to her without generating embarrassment. I was very moved by this gesture and remember asking myself "Who is this man"? Soon after, we would start dating, and commenced a much needed new beginning in both our lives. I loved and lived with this man for over 25 years and got to know him deeply.

Chet found inspiration for his writings and paintings through his extensive readings during his youth and while pursuing his studies in English Literature followed by a Doctorate in Arts and a PhD in Literary Criticism giving him full credentials as an expert in criticism, which he loved! He accumulated extensive knowledge in literature, philosophy, music, science, evolution and science fiction, as it is evident in his poems. His intellectual capacity was enormous as was his sense of humor and sensitivity.

Chet read religious volumes voraciously, from several versions of the *Bible* to the *Bagavadgita* to the *Torah* to the *Egyptian Book of the Dead*. He taught comparative religions at the University of Oregon and the University of Texas Pan-American, and in his private moments he was on an ongoing metaphysical journey. These readings propelled his unstoppable search for the meaning of life, underscoring that metaphysics and mortality are recurring themes in his poetry. You will also get a glimpse of Chet's passion for the evolution of man, as expressed in colorful humor in "The Swordfishes' First Saturday Night Ashore" and "The Far Afarensis."

Chet's attraction to "textured music," which he classified as 'transcendental', extended from early Hindi ragas and Judaea chants, through the classical period, jazz, modern music and post-modern opera, as exemplified by his favorite Jazz composer, Phillip Glass. He also enjoyed animated full-energy bands such as The Gypsy Kings, and songs like "Mac the Knife" sung by Bobby Darin, and what I call 'dark rock' like The Doors. His search for the soul of the artist was his goal. We listened to Neil Young's "Old Man" many times. I delighted in a house full of music, as it runs in my blood, too. Every day he shared musical pieces that would surprise me.

He had strong opinions about both music and paintings. His favorite artists expressed themselves in bright color, combined with nature and poignancy, such as post-Impressionists Gauguin, Hopper and Van Gogh. During our visit to Arles, he "discovered" the exact terrace and garden where Van Gogh created several of his famous scenes and Chet rejoiced! The poem "Nobody Knows the Truffles I've Seen" consolidates Chet's knowledge of piquant French phrases, which combined with his unique wit, won a first prize in the National Federation of Poetry Societies.

Chet's unique prose style was influenced by existential authors like Hemingway, Whitman, Melville, Dickinson, Emerson, Durrell, Asimov and Kerouac. He dedicated poems to many of them knowing perhaps only his professional peers would recognize his goal, like the poem "A Walk With Walt." Once, he mentioned to me how proud he felt when Isaac Asimov, a famous science fiction writer, responded to a draft to his short story "The Long Sand."

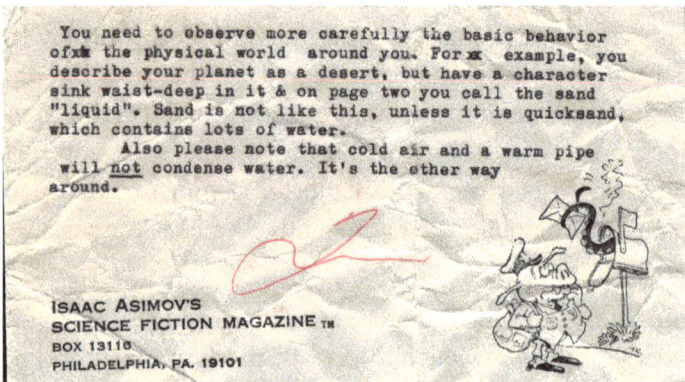

You need to observe more carefully the basic behavior ofxx the physical world around you. For x example, you describe your planet as a desert, but have a character sink waist-deep in it & on page two you call the sand "liquid". Sand is not like this, unless it is quicksand, which contains lots of water.
Also please note that cold air and a warm pipe will not condense water. It's the other way around.

ISAAC ASIMOV'S
SCIENCE FICTION MAGAZINE ™
BOX 13116
PHILADELPHIA, PA. 19101

Themes of sadness, loss and depression start manifesting themselves in Chet's poetry after the loss of his wife Anita Olsen, as in "Sere Seer," "The Old Lovers," and "The Sea Bridge Abiding." The ravages of Alzheimer's also appear in his later works.

Chet's visual art with acrylics emerged during his years in psychotherapy and provided a constructive emotional outlet. Berry Fritz, a renown painter artist and dear friend in McAllen, Tx., commented on his fabulous titles for his paintings such as "The Wizard Surrounded by a Retinue of Advisors, Sweet-talks Discontented Wife" and others.

What an honor it was to have been Chet's companion the time before and during the onset of Alzheimer's, when he often slept or seemed to be beyond the physical world. His words and wit helped him navigate the loss of memory, and he managed to pretend, pretty convincingly that he was fine! Even during that difficult period, we shared unforgettable moments of laughter and arguments over images we didn't agree on. He still had the presence of mind to say "It's a good poem if it can cause such a reaction in you."

Not everybody who is consciously aware can achieve moments of profound clarity! Yet he would write: "Life is odd, I see; we can never know is the real truth, only feel it."

As you read Chet's poems and enjoy his colorful drawings hopefully they inspire you, dear loved ones, to appreciate the importance that family and friends become in a time of veritable need. Thank you to my brother Dan, for his patience in the editing this foreword. Also, thanks to my dear friend Stella for her input. Finally, thank you to all my family for their support including, my sister-in-law Cathy and her husband Steve, my brother-in-law Jo, my dear nieces and nephews, Daren, Roger, Lexi, Ben, Taylor and the little ones, my loving sister Cristy and brother-in-law Car¬los, my brother Dan and sister-in-law Linda, my nephew Jim, my daughter Valerie and son-in-law Michael, my darling granddaughters Natalie and Abby, my son Daniel and daughter-in-law Brooke, and grandson Beckett, my nephew Rod and his wife Cynthia, and their children Rena and Sebastian for sharing your lives with Chet until the end. And special thanks to my dear friends Ana María, Michael, and Ana Michelle for your love and support, and for the editing and publishing of this anthology.

My love forever! I miss you so much!
This book is a tribute to you.

Lilly Taylor

About His Life

Chet H. Taylor was born in Glenview, outside of Evanston, Illinois on April 18, 1939. His talent for writing was spotted in junior-high school where he was allowed to skip assignments and instead write a ghost gossip sheet which would appear on the bulletin board in the hallway. He earned his MA in Creative Writing from Mexico City College (now University of the Americas). He then transferred to the University of Oregon where he earned a Doctorate of Arts and a PhD. As a teaching guest professor in Puerto Rico, Chet published several literary criticisms in the *Revista Interamericana*, Puerto Rico, 1971. Also, his article on L. Durrell's *The Alexandria Quartet* made him an expert on said novel and was published in *Modern Fiction Studies*, 1971. Other articles, short stories and poetry were published in *Corral*, 1965, *Northwest Review*, 1967-1968, *Prism International*, 1968, *Modern Fiction Studies*, 1971, *RiverSedge*, 1980, 1981, 1982. *Interstices*, 2011, 2012, *Best Austin Poetry*, 2015-2016, *Encore*, 2014, and more.

Chet's places of residence were many, but he finished his writing years in his home overlooking the Guadalupe River, in Seguin, Texas, with his wife of 25 years, Lilly Taylor. He died at the Cedar Ridge Alzheimer's Center, in Cedar Park, Texas on September 27, 2017.

Dedicated to all our family members and friends who have always stood close by...

Introduction

Chet Taylor was my brother, some eight years my senior. As a child, I remember him as intimidating but exciting, not cuddly but warm and welcoming. As a teen, I would cut my dates short to get home and watch late movies with him to hear his hilarious running dialogue about the films, peppered with sarcasm and insights and puns.

His life was exciting and filled with experiences: running a used car business while in high school, hanging out at a beatnik joint called the Purple Onion, studying in Mexico City, a little civil disobedience just before it became cool, enlisting for the Bay of Pigs before the excursion was called off, running orange groves, wheeling and dealing in Texas Río Grande Valley real estate, several marriages, teaching at Pan American University, and always, playing baseball.

He was a scholarship football player at Tulane, and I remember that he wrote a novel about a football player in New Orleans, with style influenced by Hemingway and Kerouac. It was never published, but later several of his short stories were, including "The Man Who Would not Speak to his Wife," extolling the value of words and, more importantly, the feeling behind the words. It was later still that he found his preferred voice in poetry.

His poetry runs the gamut from dark brooding on emptiness and existential despair to tender contemplation of the meaning and experience of love to just plain fun with words, my favorite genre perhaps because of the trademark amusement his sense of humor, often in the form of puns, brought his friends and family. Stricken with Alzheimer's, he wrote poignantly through it from the viewpoint of an intellect that sees but fights the dying of the light. Reading this volume was like visiting with my brother, sometimes puzzling out his complex images, sometimes laughing out loud, always amazed at the mind who created the sequence of words.

A successful real estate investor/developer, Chet nevertheless wrote poetry for half a century and a man must have a calling for poetry to do that. There is virtually no money in it and it is a struggle to get published, mostly in anthologies and submissions for juried competitions, both of which he attained. As borrowed (and paraphrased) from his poem "Visiting Gauguin in Tahiti," he was simply a poet, and poets write. The only reward is the small modicum of immortality earned by your thoughts as recorded on paper. May this endeavor help Chet Taylor to live on.

Worlds Without End

for poets are Ishmaels all

"Art of the Moby Poet" by Chet Taylor

Brain Storm

My mind started working well after forty years
so again I can work and write,
letting words twist of themselves,
dislocating language into new meaning,
while imagining in its own energy, making
written forms finite in this corpus amorphous.
Something happened: a connection somewhere:
a shard of consciousness, once free floating,
swam loose for an exquisite instant
in an equilibrium of balanced tides,
then crawled ashore from a benign saline sea.
We know best by contrasts;
long blank planes of existence
stay complete each in itself
until they eventually overlap, as
a nomad knows the desert fully
when he crosses the first fringe stubbles
and sees those weak watersigns
of the sweeping green savannas.
The senses did stir. Something did happen:

perhaps a sliver of loose star
or subtle movement of molecules,
even an errant protein,
creating a benevolent chemical balance,
even a chance shimmering of summer heat -
merely a slight cerebral accident, or maybe
a god trying to break through.
So I wrote this right away.

Art of the Moby Poet

My poems start well:
an initial idea, a single incisive image
to be developed with appropriate detail,
maybe a central metaphor about mankind
moving to a quick couplet to close
with a shift to subtle irony: so far, so good.

But something always happens
after the first smooth stanza;
images start stirring,
spin off shards of madness and metaphysics.
(There's always another layer lower).
Classical structures collapse,
metaphors get badly mixed:
the sonnet cannot hold.
Anarchy is loosed among the muses.
Onto a close-seamed sea sails a Pequod
peopled by Arabs, Ahabs, pariahs, prophets.

Madmen run amok; violent visions
ruin resolution and reason itself.
Something terribly final lurks dark and deep.

Timid lyrics are only tissue-thin lines
too slight to disturb the spirit's sleep.
What shifts is mere surface,
the fretting of an alien sentience
while its center sets dead-still,
without sentiment.

Why cast about, catching at traces?
Make the image insist, I say. Force
words to show the true face;
for only inside an awful energy
beneath this pale tallow sea.

My editor upsets easily,
resists that the solution is spiritual.
She talks of form and focus, counsels control,
but we can't resolve what we can't conceive
for primal disarray runs too deep.

Art is not submission, but search. By instinct
poets are alone and adrift on a salty sea.
A sere mirror, diffused and uninvolved
while great massings glide in huge groups
so far below, shift in mix inextricable -
spectra profundi in spiritus mundi -
flowing, but maybe not fully knowing,
for poets are Ishmaels all.

The Lungfishes' First Saturday Night Ashore

A most long long time after living
millions of years on the old seabed
for that first free oxygen so raw
like a physical blow brutally fresh.
The lungfish sank back, stunned
by the long silences between the stars.
Below, they were what the water was.
Finally they stir, ride the last of the great tide
to its farthest dying fingers; then
lobed shoulders lurched out of the old seabed,
safe from the bigteeth left in the bay behind.
A huge sun burns round and red:
its fire so full, no longer filtered.
They feel heavy, separate from the sea,
unsteady, and more alone.
Now they nibble on juicy fruits, owning the beach
as the world is for them, empty of enemies.
The rows of dunes assume truer shapes;
making them matter even more.
Terrors draw down to darker places,

to the old sea still full of bigteeth,

while somnolent lesser shapes still

mark sleep in the old seabed.

Here they are the bigteeth.

The new lords lope about so full of themselves.

All this was for them! This was theirs!

Exultant new gods began exploring their Eden.

One Last Trip

When I visit her hospital suite
we recreate our sea voyages
sailing past Indian Ocean islands
to the South China Sea, sleeping
on layered blue and yellow silks
while the sun slides over the end of the Earth,
pulling fierce orange and reds away with it.

Now I will tell her of a new voyage
to an Antarctica of immense blue icebergs,
all floating solid, even serene,
while holding the sun frozen inside.

The Sea Bridge Abiding

A wild place our planet is,
of alien certitudes long not our own:
indifferent, ever edgy, seems the sea
when flat, sunless, waiting still,
though seeming quite content
with no needs and nothing self-important,
patient as we are not
while we wait for a sauté of foie gras
to put on our shelled oysters, fleshy
and sensual, faintly throbbing before the sizzle.
We eat the sea and sometimes the sea eats us.

Maybe the ocean's always aware in its own way,
often pulling itself easily back in indifference,
letting red eyes of bonfires flare for eager lovers
while in the far heavens starscape carnivals
go on forever: what the Gopi milkmaids saw
when they looked deep into Krsna's eyes.

Many sleep, lulled by an easy surf,
the moon in calm tidal pools without wrinkles.
Later a thick sea fog may settle all into itself
as it comforted us when we first
crawled ashore on lobed fins
after waiting for our air bladders
that once stabilized us in the depths
to evolve into lungs pulling in raw air
with its own trace of salt.
We often come back to be near
where we once so long were, for
it is forever and we are not.

Little Lily at First Light

I have loved two wives:
Anita long dead and Lily still long alive.
They both stay in my head all day.
It's nice to have something;
even the pain was better than nothing.
It's still a long life
with its taste of ecstasy in memory
though that sense of inevitable loss
seeming always to underlie all.

But, sometimes she says
I'm too rambunctious in bed, though
seems to appreciate the attentions.
All night long my hands feel her body close,
at morning find such a sweet face,
that won my heart in the first place.

I try to keep our world together a little longer,
for everything leaves one way or the other.
It's a lucky old man who has a love still left.

The Three Phases of Eve

The Image: once a real woman, I'm sure,
she arose, dripping from a warm salty sea;
a mermaid water-born, beyond real flesh,
old secrets soon forgot by short lives
linked on a long timeline
to a larger purpose not her own.
How deep these tracings of desire?
As we peel the psyche of species layers
the stubborn patterns remain ever set
in alien, insistent, sensual intent.
Wild flung hair, clothes on a chair;
the purpose is not our purpose
but points to layers that tell a single truth:
the heart of life is simply life again.
There is really only one woman:
she arose as eros as a rose.
I have always been a friend to flowers --
ah, yes, fulsome wenches in frumpled beds:
Rangoon in monsoon, silvery moon, ah June!

The Ideal: she arose from a sheer, reflective sea,
a mirror maid was she,
the sun still shining on her skin
but which is she, which the sea?
The psyche makes its own shapes:
the songs she sings are songs of my self.
The old gods want too much worship;
I must reach past the time-worn tracings
to find out who she really is.
I can't get there from here.

The Actual: a real woman to be sure,
she rises from a sullen, clouded sea,
a mere maid, after all,
a part of the sea, yet apart,
not golden as she seemed in the sun.
She stands rested and ready to run,
clearly in no mood for monkey business.
"It is not the face of Eve you see,"
says she, "but your own, those of old Adam.
We are truly coming to know
what we have not known:
you have a long way to go; even so,
we can simply live and choose to love."`

Lovers Have a Year of Haikus

finally it's spring
i watch a new butterfly
simply flutter by

skin gold in summer
then red in the late sunlight
she came in colors

something in us is
like those high thin autumn clouds
being not being

i saw the year through
high mists come and go then snow
it's my last season

in the spring we leaf
in summer grow and fall slow
in winter we leave

follow the seasons
to the very end to find
your love waits again

A Long Way Back

I brought her my joy but she's dead now
so some things I have to take back.
We know somewhere beyond feeling
that all loves will be lost.
Take the body, if you wish
but leave the feelings, for
she will grow no older, always
be the age she last was.
She was here and the she wasn't.

Long ago she was lean and loose-limbed
sprawling about the bed;
then her hair was so thin
he could feel the skull under her skin
as he holds her, hoping to die with her
to make sure she'll be all right.

Sometimes now I see a woman
smart with a good sense of things,
so I know the world is still open.

Am I a sad poet just saying what oft was thought
but ne'er so poorly expressed?
The first to come back were the words and colors.
I had forgotten the world can surprise.

If we touch each other
maybe still exists a place
of meeting, of merger, where
the sea and sky seal without seam.

Visiting Gauguin in Tahiti

Wife and children faded away,
sad small ghosts left behind:
as did those huddled in winter coats.
He had to go where the colors were.
Gauguin found his new world in the Marquesas,
a place to put down those colors on canvas
that filled his head so fierce and insistent.
He knew at once his world was here,
in this wild garden that lifted life beyond itself,
a perfect place to paint.

A native woman ground poi, kept the lepers away.
The painting went easily and well
with canvases shipped back to Paris markets.
Gaugin became an instant celebrity in absentia,
but money meant little except passage and paint.
Paris was seeing his sensual images in raw colors,
feeling the jungle greens, bright sun, brown flesh.
He was simply a painter and painters paint.

Gauguin died there of syphilis and dementia.
His last works were dominated by black,
the final canvas a somber winter scene of home.
Seeing a way to see we'd been long without,
he willingly gave up what he was
to become something more.
He did what had to be done,
asking no one else to understand.
Everything ends, at last even the light.
Island authorities found him on the floor.
We come and go away; his colors stay.

Love Long Ago

My wife grew older with me for awhile;
we stayed lovers in our own, easy way,
though she said little about this, for
young people think it's funny
when hair is thin and skin not so smooth.
Always we knew that everything
would end badly, for everything always does.

A commissioned painting of her shows
a smiling beauty in her own backyard
as the lattice breaks sunlight about her
while the shadows are softening into dusk,
the diffused light catching her sense of grace.
Memory always mixes in:
her eyes were brown, brown,
with a way soft of looking around.
The sun finds those eyes,
and her necklace jewelry stones,
the reflections bent at just the right slant
mirroring sadness, somehow, in a happy face.

Illusions abound in that image
as if she knew some secrets.

Then I remember again when
she wasn't a painting.

The Old Haikuist No Longer Sleeps Well

haikus go at things
see this as a simple world
hard to understand

empty men sleep badly
his wife died in the winter
the world is so thin

winter is a world
with only still fogs and ghosts
left to remember

the mountain quiet
is more than ice and dead sticks
something much thinner

a high mountain bare
I´m glad she was once happy
valley full of fog

A Far Afarensis

We followed ourselves finally back to here:
an African rainforest three million years ago,
now hard-scrabble desert sliced into grey gullies
by old floods. We walk these washes, checking
the raw, layered walls like supermarket shoppers
for old bones. Each age erratically seamed,
the past shows a fitful pattern.
Only skeletons are left as the rest rots away.
A hard time coming we had of it, for
border guards were bribed, permits negotiated;
the native bearers had to be watched
while absent wives and children grow up alone.
The past disappears behind us also.

We worked in pairs towards the mountains.
Mon dieu, cried Andre who espied
in the ravine side A. Afarensis -- our ape.
He's waited for us a long time.

We picked with dentist tools, taking off
the mineral salts with basting brushes.
Three weeks later, it emerged four feet tall,
an apparition arising from ancient earth:

the left leg bones lost, and some ribs --
jackals or hyenas foraging for juicy marrow.
Paleontologists are patronizing sorts,
so we awkward academics called it 'Adam'.
Missing links are not monsters; shifts are subtle:
old apes do look alike; but this is us.

Yet the matter runs even deeper;
maybe memory is buried beyond the bone:
Adam's own ancestors -- the earliest mammals --
scratching, scared in the rocks like small rats
by huge shadows of scaled leathered wings
lacking still the lightness of feather.
A squealing frenzy of fears sweeps the heart;
nothing is safe, nothing free, except the burrow --
good wetsmelling sweet dirt surround.
Ah, forgotten already the shadows rolling above,
riding updrafts from a hot world of new wounds
coasting on a constant continuum of air
stretching unbroken before and after;
we will never know that.

These badlands, cold and clear at night,
such awful saharas between stars,
only distances, always distances, and things lost.
At least Adam now sleeps in the open with us.

The Angels All About Ward B

He died, he shouldn't have, but he did.
Yet it was not over for her.
She knew the fates would shift
a universe of infinities for them.

She knew little of the real way of things,
though everything has to be somewhere,
so anything lost will finally be found:
soon they would be one again.
Space and time are not limits, just measures.
If the love is already in her heart,
no absence could be forever,
for everything always exists, somewhere.

In dreams he held her as lights danced for them
under evolving autumn auroras.
They watched, lying on green hillsides,
he holding her through the warm night
in a world without end, with realities infinite.
He was Ulysses returning; she Penelope waiting,
knowing the promise he must come.

She waited for her wanderer;
her Ulysses was coming home, nearing.
If she had not this hope
sorrow would be unceasing.
She felt the universe shifting
to give her heart what it had to have.

Sere Seer

She quit talking, withdrew into herself,
so finally we left her alone,
bedridden on the second floor,
but overlooking the desert.

The first thin reed of dawn starts
filling in faded grays and finding clouds.
The wind changes. Sand shifts,
taking the easiest shape.
A rare rain surprises the dry earth
down to where color doesn't really matter.

The sun runs its long curve, leaving
the last light rich in unreal reds,
burnished in deep Byzantine golds,
burning until the long alkali flats and low sky
resolve life and death in a closed seam.
The giant wheel turns a degree: another world
as we watch, willing to be distracted.

Thin air empties the night,
hardens stones and chills the heart
because the heart is not enough and we're alone.
We cannot find faces in the sands,
but only the desert in ourselves.
Despite summer memories of lost lovers,
the heart and the stone and the night
become one with the cold.
And all are desert, forever desert,
turning always in tides of changing light.

One day she is gone,
gone into the desert for good.

Lost But Not Gone

People with Alzheimer's disease know, but others
don't, how it is to forget. Memory goes away little
by little, like where you live and how to get there,
anything past or planned. If you keep walking
on a sidewalk you may end up in the woods.
Memory is money in the bank though I can never
use it. The past is gone. I can tell immediately
when someone knows me or not, meaning whether
or not I have to tell him I have Alzheimer's.
On everyday topics like the weather I'm okay and
can talk easily. People are interested and like if
I make a few jokes. It relaxes them if they can laugh
and kid around. Often I tell someone I know
all his secrets but don't worry because I can't
remember them. I remind them now they can use the
same jokes again though probably do that anyway.
I carry around my name, address, and phone number.
Never have I forgot my name but I told
my wife that the other info comes in handy.
I write this page all at one time, or I'd forget what's

written and have to start all over. You got to use what you got, I guess, until someday you'll forget who you are. My wife sometimes asks me who she is and I still know and say so, making a small joke like 'well, you were my wife yesterday.' She likes that and things get normal for a while and I'm glad I had enough sense to marry her. I told her that today and she cried but told me not to worry for she was happy. If she's happy then everything's okay. At least I still know that I am. Soon nothing will be in my head because I'm not dying, I'm disappearing.

The Inquisition Questions Its First Pagan

You torture for nada, Torquemada.
Have you never suspected the truth of things?
The earth gathers up its own rosebuds,
remembering all easily
while you clutch fears so close;
we live in a grace of incompletion
so to introspect, and even suspect.
Our bounties are well-cached,
all seeing from a single soul.
Have you truly never suspected?

Things feel broken inside,
always the stink of bowels.
Red pools swell on dirty stones
 shimmering oddly in their own light.
These damned fanatics of blood and death!
Their emptiness becomes us all.
We are crippled by this winter country
 where our single soul is stretched so thin.
I was curious; I came to see,
never knowing that we

were what they feared most:
the ghosts of pagans still about.

My wife will look for me a long time,
never to know more than I never came back.
(Her black hair barely dents the pillow.)
So hard to let go of life,
I would rather die in warmth.
If only it were summer.

Which Is She, Which The Sea

One day early in June she came right up to him
as he painted the with sun mirroring off the bay.
He watched her become colors herself in low light
as she posed in the dunes while the sea stole
its colors from the sky, becoming its own mosaic
always shifting, no longer solid-blue with faint
gauzy clouds between being and not being
before aging swiftly to serious gold,
a Byzantine bronzing, the stuff of treasure troves
and holy cities changing into something to touch.
He could not always see which was sea, which she,
in shifting hues exotic, erotic in an easy anarchy.

They lay together in day's end
before the moon took all the light.
We can live with the sun as one of us,
we can only wonder at the stars, blooming
in starfields' centuries and light years away:
so many secrets still around us.
Finally the light was gone; the painting over.

He came back to the beach in late November,
the strong summer colors now long gone;
the waves crunched in, hissing, then fell back
sighing as he walked along the beach
watching for her everywhere.
The muted sun was only a gray ghost
and sea and sky merged seamless.
The gallery showing had been a huge success.
Critics called her "The Woman in the Dunes."

She was lost to him. Someday there might be a nudge;
she would simply say, "Remember me?"
She might come back as he did.
Which was she, which the sea? Just she.

Nobody Knows the Truffles I've Seen

Too soon for feasting, smile and wait awhile,
don't peek at the soufflé,
or all its puff goes away.
After all, the burgundy must breathe,
easy now: strong stuff, strong stuff.
Let the last run of sugar scoot
right onto the ripening fruit.
Select subtle spices from a cupboard shelf,
it'll strip slowly layers from any covered self
for a rose is arroz is eros.

Anticipation is nice with preparations precise;
a heavy pâté, a light soufflé,
champagne -- a Moët, I would say --
chilling in an oaken bucket on a tray
as wet beads slide down the side and away.
Trout Marguery, a Provençal chardonnay,
don't quaff half a carafe;
it's quite a blunder and you'll go asunder.
Parisian mousse, loose talk of Toulouse:

well, nuncle, this plainly will do!
Under high-ceilings we whisper among
dark polish and rainbows of light in the night
as life blooms filling the rooms
(truly a pro's prose apropos our pose).

After slow coffee and powdered toffee,
even some Courvoisier, perhaps Grand Marnier,
don't rush her or you'll create a fluster
for passion is the most we can muster
against life's coming decay,
so delay the dénouement, delay.

You sense the secret, finally exalted:
life is delicate, easily exhausted --
yet so dear, this thin veneer, as
even the basics lie beyond us.
La sauce c'est tout.

The Same Seas, Often Seen

A softer sea tonight, often seen:
the surface swimming now in Byzantine bronze,
a skim of taut shimmering thin skin
stretching and loosening. A singularity stirs
as somnolent low waves lull us away
from the soft waters weaving and reweaving,
dissolving the illusion of lines.
An artistic seascape tonight, aesthetically seen,
drags along cloud smears in silent violent
letting red dust from dead deserts cause colors:
golds hammered fine from collapsed constructs
once full of pompous plans and great purpose
as reviewed in the last gradients of solid blues.
An older sea tonight ominously seen
as the sun touches the sea
sailboats are shadowed by dark daggered fins
as seabirds panic, dive towards a dark shore.
A track of worn pilings trace into open ocean
sketching a lost curve of things:

the skeleton of some immense meaning.
A seamless sea today softly seen:
a sensuous warmth swells the seawater,
rises around, surrounds the senses,
dilutes the daiquiris, diffuses our narrow lives
as the waters gather themselves, perhaps
protein chains will combine, enzymes interact,
letting free-floating cells colonize.
A sentient sea tonight, suspiciously seen:
skimming white reefs of skulls and blanched bone
mulling new beasties to march over the mudflats,
perhaps to peruse the shallow tide pools
recombining in a collective consciousness,
mingling single memories among all memory.
A changing sea tonight, newly seen:
things are known through us;
something lies beyond; so
take these connections, I say;
a man may know more than he thinks
in this ubiquitous sea, always seen.

Life Always Ends Alone

In bed we're a pair of old, weary lovers
hanging onto each other under the covers,
with much bravura neither of us is sure of.
Sometimes she calls me a 'ragtag scalawag',
and even a galoot, to boot.
Gone are the days of wine and poses
as we seep in our bones of aged animals.

Her hair thin in my old hands
slips through like silk wisps.
Life's worn out now
so it's best to just pretend
a pervasive sadness doesn't underlay all.

In winter's monolith it's easier to feel an end.
Death takes so much.
Now this old ghost wakes alone
never to find her ever again;
it's better to have no one at all
than someone to always miss.

Maybe love lives longer than lovers?
People at the park may someday wonder
where those two gray ghosts have gone,
those ones that always seemed so real.

Old Dreams of Once

I came alone. I always come back alone.
The courtyard was still full of last year's leaves,
in left-alone pockets out of the wind.
A few bruise-bellied clouds still hung low,
so heavy they must rain to rise again.

Her footsteps once were crisp in the courtyard
amid the rustle of leaves and windchimes,
a light run of random single notes, each separate
in itself, cascading in surprised spontaneous rushes:
unending interplays, subtle ways to feel, while
dwindling with the breeze to slow symphonies,
not of chords but staggered notes
seeming to understand silence.

I remembered where we once were,
where she, so thin-boned, had waited for me,
feeling thunder as summer skies split open.
In a rustle of rain and soft silks,
I would watch her brush her hair out

sitting bedside, a frozen image fixed forever.
I wanted those nights to stay whole worlds.
Sometimes the wind opened the clouds
for a full moon, causing the candlelight to waver
and curtains to stir in the new morning.
Wet light was left where her ashes were spread;
soon my own would join hers.

In death, we might find each other
as Spring snowmelt runs down to the river
and currents rub gently, slowly against soft banks.
Maybe she'd surprise him in the first bouncing rapids
letting each tumble over and around the other
until the river runs to a common sea,
to the Indian Ocean where the fish could fly,
or maybe to the South China Sea
where beaches were pink and black.
She would even show him the South Pole
where blue icebergs hold the sun frozen forever.

That Obscure Objet of Desire

There is really a reason for a naked lady
who eagerly accepts full sun and ecstasy
as lovers engorge in eager embrace
with each depending on the other.
This is when they can imagine
themselves not alone, feeling
that 'yes' that is deeper than any dissent
as apparent anarchy is loosed.
White may contain all the colors
but we still relish the full rainbow.
We broach all order, go beyond even it's idea.
Chiaroscuro obscure in a dark caroche,
right here the mask seems thinnest,
where the secret's so easily seen,
and my wife is the first and final woman.
Well, nuncle, it's only natures' way
to make people out of people.
There is a reason for a naked lady
for beauty seems its own answer.

A new evening breeze lifts the canopies,
shifts whole banks of ill-organized leaves.
A lady spreads herself lightly on her own white sheets
with lanky limbs sprawling akimbo in disarray
seeming a leopard lounging in a sun-scorched jungle.
A look of love drifts from her shadowed eyes
thus demanding all attention.
Such images run deep in the DNA
for ancient gods too have been there
to find an intense reality, another world
exotic and erotic, ever insistent,
with its own truth of pleasure and treasure.
Sometimes we do suspect there is a real truth.
The universe, the species, even the sexes
all evolved by splitting, fragmenting, recombining,
with mutation the real wildcard.
Let's face it: subjectivity overrides objectivity
though never is it the thing itself.
Yes, there really is a reason for a naked lady.

Señor Romántico Addresses the Afterglow

Frieda suggests, after pinot noir and pâté,
skinny-dipping in the backyard pool:
both kids at college and the fence is high.
So why not? Something within us always wants
to break forms and live lives of feeling.

Frieda floats so lightly, lithely
languorous in a warm seamless sea.
Her muted ferocity seems fragile,
yet far from death and dust.
Broken gardenia blooms float in the pool skim,
browned and redolent, heavy with musk.
Cloying petals cling around her,
an old Eden still endures.

She dissembles on purpose, of course.
Now chaos must again work itself out:
the leopard leaps from a low branch
out of a subconscious canopy clouded
in sliding shadows and ancient light,
a mottled mélange of many meanings

remembering the jade-green rainforest
of red meat and mate.
The rush always surprises us.

Spent waves slosh insolently into tiled gutters,
the tired salmon sun rests on a last rim of light
layering the pool in pink, then red, then night
Frieda lies close in feral refraction.
We no longer know what it meant;
new auroras need new aborigines.
We sense some elusive absolute overlays all,
we hold onto that promise as she murmurs,
"Señor Romántico is still analyzing the afterglow?"
Still a missing world rests ever
at the farthest end of unremembered memory.

Onomatopoeia for Lovers

Sounds like lovers sensually align,
become soft sublime metaphors themselves
slipping into each other in rows,
beautiful as a star-deep night
sensuous sibilant sounds well beyond prose,
letting everything connect in easy continuum.

Poems carry feelings too, you know:
sex and sensuality can be slippery, even amorphous,
but don't toss in the towel, use another vowel.
I would say anything to win the woman I want,
why not a tender entreaty,
with no sharp edges or abrupt stops,
so use your own muse, spend the day
where all things end up together in play,
just a long intimate song luffing easily along:
"I see, mon amie, I see
you are the easy breeze in an airy lea,
the cause of a heart's ennui when you're away."

Let her feel the words by their resonance;
the hiss and swoosh of an ancient sea,
the slow, sliding flow of the ageless Aegean
insinuate some joie de vivre
(just say it and you'll see):
Ah, onomatopoeia, my love is she!

The soothing consonance rocks us
as esses wait for vowels
to make dreams again.

The Dead Poet's Wife

He's gone for good so I'll have
to make myself a self again.
He never called us a married couple;
we were always mates.
We created new places in our hearts
just to have them hollow back out.

We both had bad early marriages
never completely left behind
as we lived together, wary only at first,
ever trying to find the right words.
He held onto me in bed,
so we forgot or forgave all before.

Once he wrote a poem about me
titled "A Pro's Prose Apropos Her Pose."
He knew he was always safe
if he could make me laugh.
Now the bed is so empty
even when I'm in it.

I cry some when I feel me in his poems,
though now I try to write my own.
He told me once to relax,
let the poem tell you where to go.
If he were here he would
want to edit it, rewrite it his own way.
No way! My memories are mine!

Then the fog came into his head.
He told me I was the reason
he tried to stay around so long.
He wrote his own goodbye.
He wanted to go off alone, I guess,
an old Eskimo on an ice floe.

His first wife died young and the sadness
was sometimes like a ghost.
Everybody loses everyone, that's why
we hold on until all wears out.

I can't say things like he could
but maybe I felt them even more.
We always knew someone had to go first;
I'm glad it was he;
he wouldn't have done well alone.
Life lets us be for a little while
before we're lost again in ever.

Coals of Old Fires

the only mercy
will be forgetting that once
I could remember

Finally he came back, found her married.
But her legs had gone bad;
so she didn't move around much.
He showed them how to order
crutches from the general store
paying for them himself
so she was up and about again.
But he never came back.
We all always want to feel
we're where we want to be, yet
yesterday is often, long gone
and tomorrow may never come.
Once he wanted to be there;
but now emptiness was the enemy.

After the Divorce

We ate our last meal together
then left the restaurant,
both alone now, letting
life become suddenly bittersweet,
wondering if the sun would ever
again see us together, maybe
letting us hang around each other a bit.
Someday she might walk back in,
someday she might. She might.

Pain is pain, it's true,
but pain is life too.
We never knew this life wouldn't stay,
but sometimes all simply wanders away.
Divorce is like a death
for we wonder how we'll never touch
as the days slow and gray,
with our lives so far away.
Memory will become suspect,
alone in its own forever,
with empty spaces, empty places.

One day one will hear of the other's death,
and not know how to feel.
We'll have to pretend that a sadness
doesn't underlie all.

The Raga Cycle of Life

A few photons, just the faintest
get through first. The sun
comes round to climb again, already
readying the ragas for those that can't remember.
At first light sounds a faint chord
inside the drone of harmonium.
A soft and steady sitar oversees new stirrings
while a percussive tabla, unhurried,
reaches the drowsy senses, so the line
between sleeping and waking becomes indefinite,
thus begin the soft remonstrations of morning
reminding this is the real world:
a no-nonsense place of focus, of maintenance
which works in a simple straight line
with time to prepare faces and plant seeds,
make breakfast and plan midday meals.
Discreet dawn colors slide from a fresh sun,
diffuse the misty sky into layers of reds
letting thousands of sea mirrors deceive as one.
So we assume a self, just like the sea.
Such is the way of the new day.
The slow dance of the first day began
when A. afarensis looked with Adam in awe:

being before the idea of being.
Sun shadows swept over fresh grasses,
over the green hills as far as one could see:
all seem mixed in a blue-green Miró
while we become men of sun, men of day.

Heat burns deep and hard
with a terrible desert star staring close,
a fierce, spinning fire that burns
down to elementals, fundamentals.
Now the notes strike solid and sure;
pulses are strident, percussive-
hot and quick, harsh and hard.
The living hunker down to survive:
variations on a narrower theme now
as the tablas are heavy and steady,
even insistent, without any asides.
Now is the time of raw necessity;
 shovels sweat even survival.
 Well, we found we could climb
 those golden Byzantine columns,
 for light itself is the ultimate answer
 as energy and matter are the same.
 The day is long and without thought
 until the sun at last lets up,
 then time is beyond the day.
 Wrenched colors resolve on the horizon
 in the last nuances of late afternoon as
 a salmon sun seems shoaled on black mountains.

The last seabirds streak for shore:
sharp black stilettos in a muting skyscape
of reds and orange, almost angry.
They come in as one, slanting as one,
falling into the shore, one now with the darkness
with no separations, seamless;
like light itself, both empty and all.
The day ends in explosion of tabla and sitar.
Then all is still and seems gone.
It is evening.

Hard men of light get lost at night, unsure
what they see are phantasms or avatars amorphous.
A dark wind comes up, blows loose clouds about.
A new moon hangs fresh over tiled roofs,
floats on rivers carrying sun to the sea.
Sinewy elves so stubborn and sure
dilate in this dance of starlight,
knowing now of new worlds
layered even inside light itself.
Evening reverberates in sympathetic adagio
then appasionato as a resonating oneness
invites us to become gods and play all parts
with chords becoming something set free,
bending notes, warping sound as it is played,
showing nothing is alone for all is One,
part of a slow pulsing overlaps of purpose,
a oneness where each overlap the other:
desire and completion in their own metaphysic.

The men feel their women open to them
as each self extends joining
the erotic fervor of the frenzied sitar
seizing the fierce climax, foreordained forever.
We are the song around us as
our new lenses see beyond the outer ether
nineteen billion lightyears away a solid wall
of stars and worlds, and we know
that light is life and we are light
as a final recognition overfloods all:
the self is one with all else.
While the moon clears low clouds,
climbs now familiar old columns
to blooming nascent nexi and white dwarfs,
as separates blur and shapes slide away
solids and shadows seem the same
making each instant ever, and all is one.
 The lone drone holds a long single tone:
 Shantih. Shantih. Shantih.

A Little Savoir Faire Gets the Poet There

As solving her utter resistance
calls for ultra-insistence
so he scaled her towers by sending flowers
until fair lady was his.
'Bonjour, monsieur', said she
as he fell to a knee, insuring
a future of such repartee,
never making any reference 'to the grave'
and knowing a true poet
never adds 'Burma Shave'.

The best at writing of loss
is some select eclect all alone
who remembers the time when
something was, then wasn't.
Like yahoos yelling across the cosmos
so something will know we're here,
poets leave scribbled last words too,
possibly daydreaming posthumous publication,
or like old tourists visiting tombstones,

remembering when the table was set for two,
holding deserts and just desserts.

Once the doctor's office left word
saying my wife's test
showed no cancer after all.
I told her now life
would be better than we feared.
She said tonight would be
better than I could hope.

Since shadows do thicken, perhaps
something more is coming,
maybe a memory of the long-before
that the spirits won't show as we
linger always on their dark edge.
We have to love what we will
to make anything worth the while.
I would rouse my wife to talk of this
but she doesn't wake well.

A Full Philip Glass for Us All

Reality plays its cards in continuum constant
as life is the motion of moments where
some musicians let lasting sounds go slow
so a conundrum not humdrum recurs, while
fresh notes are added like new kids on the block
as 'hello, hello, what feeling are you in'
asks Glass darkly, again and again
while differences seem softer, more subtle
in a lyricism of the relentless, the endless
where beauty is bare like a lovely woman,
for if space were empty it wouldn't be at all,
the sadness of consciousness so contained
wanting to break out and run in the rain
like some old guy stretching his soul
thus repeating everything to keep all whole
and the current ever-constant bringing
life and death forever together
as the pall and the call become all
with division definite, measures well measured
leaving an unending memoir of someday

when the table was set for two,
a relentless revival no need to rehearse
in this ever art of slow silences and verse,
as reality repeats itself in continuum constant.

The Old Lovers See Spring Again

We are a species conscious of coming death,
that last touché that touches all.
We often lie, my lady and I, on our lawn,
as a late May night presages summer.

The music can be felt, disappearing,
then returning, recombined in new chords,
softer ragas of the evening bend notes in mid-play
from a sitar with its own erotic will
feeling one with all the sensuous spectra.

We have infinity all around us
as sweeps of sky and starscapes,
carpets of galaxies sprawl out without end.
Nothing is fixed, nothing ever final;
everything is a mere part of all.
As space curves in on itself
like lovers each unto the other
as low waves roll onto white beaches
over coral reefs combing them into lace,

letting seasons fall naturally into place,
while each end of the earth stays white with ice.

We hear only a train whistle deep in the darkness
reminding us we are here and alone together,
its notes leaving little but a vapor trail spread so thin
in a place where finally only the subjective is real.
The universe echoes the resonance
of some grand drum somewhere
beating like our own hearts.

A Blind Date

My ordinary expectation of perceiving shapes in space
without touching them was wondrous to her.
She knew it was not good to envy seers
so from then on I was casual in filling her in
about the ordinary things each day,
not as some guide but including my own ideas,
little by little describing things
like the darker rainclouds when we hurry
as dusk is coming with late sun shining off the seawater
and she felt the heat on her face.
She said her favorite mental images were the pinpoints
when I would describe far stars in the night sky,
where no one's ever been before.
She sensed my frustrations of not knowing.

When we first became lovers
she said she was so nervous
until I told her the night was dark for both of us,
so we'd have to feel our way together,
with the sun on our faces in the morning.

Getting the Girl

Around his love an immense fence of defense
hence any lover best approach undercover
for faint will will ill-fill fair lady so
refrain from uttering and sputtering or stuttering
as this known bon vivant and cunning linguist
just wants to hold his love and kiss forever,
staying away from humdrum conundrums
or phlegmatic fanatics and picky pedantics
for memory always fades into
a Miró mosaic of unfinished images
stretching without end around fate's bends
trying to create a coherent continuum
after seeing her sideglance to be askance
as she considered his malarkey more anarchy
though his poetry and prose pose
sheepishly wearing new emperor's clothes,
oozing sadness that infuses the pain with ennui
citing lovelorn lovers kept apart, you see,
for faint art ne'er wins fair lady
though a soft sonnet on it declaiming in passion

will oft times carry the day away,
for the overeager heart easily exudes excess
and it won't digress, just hope for the best
for sometimes we see clearly life is erratic,
loose-ended so let her wander today
through verbiage, as one at a buffet
finding just the right way to say, while
letting will and sonnets sway her his way.

Melville and Fayaway, Faraway

Always remembering his young years at sea,
though outgrowing a sailor's ways,
Melville, working for years in a customs house,
took to wife a proper churchwoman
from a family nervous about her seaman husband
who knew much of things beyond the Good Book.

His wife minded her marital duties;
never asked about the South Seas.
All had read Typee, about cannibals and sin,
published and quite popular before Moby Dick
for Fayaway and pagan amorality caused quite a stir.

His wife, a plain woman in formless dresses,
had a certain sad half smile,
when she first saw him yesterday after work,
her sadness only fully gone
when she spoke of the children.
She once surprised him by asking
if she would ever have his heart.

After working at the Port Authority the next day
he walked the long way to the winter docks
where cold mists roil among the anchored ships,
a long cold winter of ice and slate skies.
The harbor freeze leaves in late spring;
as mangos and fruits start arriving from the Indies.
As always on the pier he looks southward
over that long, warming curve of seawater,
thinking of Fayaway so hopelessly far away.

Melville first saw the Marquesas as sea mountains,
seemingly lost in an unending blue-banded Pacific:
volcano cones surrounded by coral reefs
under vast dark-bellied cloudscapes holding rain.
During the night he slipped over the ship´s side
finding a village of palmleaf huts
where brown women, as soft as ripe fruits,
welcomed the new sailor from the cold climes.

Right away he found the slender Fayaway;
They were together from the first moment.
She laughed, covering him with flowers
while waves ran around them.
The days stretched out, leisure unhurried;
their bodies seamed together on green reed mats.

They put pasty poi in each other's mouth,
ate pineapple, coconuts, breadfruit, bananas.
Soft Polynesian syllables sounded between them
while a rustling of waves kissed sand.
The months went on and on without counting.

Back on shipboard another sailor had said
the natives were cannibals; suspicious,
he searched around and found a sack of skulls.
Thereafter, the Typees kept a close eye on him.

One day a Dutch longboat came into the bay.
He sprinted over the beach and swam,
thrown spears flying all around.
He was pulled in and signed on
to a whaler leaving Nukuheva harbor
that had lost two men hunting whales.
That quickly Fayaway was left far behind.

He knew never would he ever see her again.
A last light had lingered over the fading islands
like a long wavering goodbye
as late seabirds streaked to shore, hurling
dark bodies through the new night,
Fayaway forever lost in the last light.

She still lived for him, forever lying
always in those red blossoms.
For years the loss had lain inside him,
a heavy stone in the heart.
Joy and sadness are naturally mated,
turning over and over like the Earth and tides
while rivers keep running to the seas,
and Ahabs want to strike behind the mask,
as Ishmaels cling to floating coffins.

His wife met him in the town square
for the walk home. He took her hand in his,
then told her that her husband loved her.
She turned away but kept his hand.
He couldn't tell if she was crying.
He told her his new book was about a whale.
They walked home together.
Things get lost. Things get found again.

When the last sunlight and colors are gone
the starfields come out of nothing
and sometimes is seen the face of forever
like a long uninterrupted dream.

Children of the Sun, Ghosts of the Moon

Maybe sleep opens old secrets
as dreams touch true anarchy
when nightwinds angle off the roof,
for time never was until a movement of matter
finally stirred in the still,
finally insisting on its perception.

Just as love needs to know death
let the species' will find its own reality
as evolution proceeds apace,
sensing, perhaps, ourselves as seeds,
beginnings of a new species
capable of conceptualizing its own ends
even while struggling with a survival agenda
while the dead merely wait, maybe knowing all.

Children of the sun sometimes,
also often we're ghosts of the moon
still trying to discover ourselves
on the logical premise that

there is an answer for everything.
Science and Einstein have established
that matter and energy are
ultimately the very same
since energy is only mass at higher speed
(when asked how he knew,
Einstein said simply "the math works').

Now the new String Theory's math establishes
that nothing itself doesn't exist
for the universe is indeed not empty at all,
carrying within it everywhere
strands of subatomic energy bonding together,
suggesting even a timeless
singular consciousness of sorts
which might mean nothing need ever be lost.

Even the dead may wait in their own way,
though I still hold my wife in bed,
knowing we may live in a universe
which overlaps our own consciousness,
suggesting we could always be together
if physics and metaphysics ever met forever.

The Old Guy Holds On

Like many old men, something
slips away when I sleep,
when I awaken I have to remember who I am.
My feet have little feeling;
blood doesn't move well anymore.
The bottoms of my feet are always cold.

I wake these nights to find
my wife a small curve inside my big curve;
such intimacies mix easily with memory.
I move slow fingers over her head:
feeling how faint is the slight hair, so silken.
Her bones are thin, maybe easily broken:
for the nature of all is to fall apart.
The first morning light
  means I have her for another night.
  In these lesser times we cling together,
  understanding why one mate often
  dies off so soon after the loss of the other.

No more anarchy of summer thunderstorms,
dry leaves tap on winter windows.
Someday no one will be here.
She asks me how would I find her?
Maybe we just disappear into some darkness,
but I'm not going to tell her that.
We know now what we were afraid to know:
soon no one will be there to care.

Edward Hopper: Light Alone

At first we see only crude blocks of color,
in a style so plain without apology.
Maybe a bit boring, rather primal
though holding a tension and repressed emotion.
Hopper found a sad and simple beauty –
and made it work his way,
seeing an ennui in the stiff figures,
sensing sadness in those shadows.

In Hopper's best-known painting, Nighthawks,
he sits a silent couple on stools
in an early a.m. diner clean and well-lighted,
somewhere not to be alone or out there where
their own footsteps sounded on the cement
as cold winds wound through dark alleys.

The café is quiet, motion minimal.
The people inside are part of the place.
Hopper's flattened lines feel static, sad;
here lives are starkly still.

Customers stare into coffee cups, look into laps.
Maybe once the couple had talked of love;
now they sit still and quiet, not touching,
neither grieving nor talking,
not wanting to listen to their own loneliness,
resigned to being settled and safe for now,
glad not to go home where they're all alone.

Hopper's art is overtly blunt.
His truths are hard ones, not softened nor lyrical:
a sadness of people in shadows.
In one of his last paintings,
Sun in an Empty Room, a bare room is open
to the sun streaming in from outside:
a good place for living and dying.
Everywhere fills with a golden wonder.
Hopper once said all he wanted to do
was paint light on the side of a house.

A Mexican Dream

With only a high school diploma
she drove out of Mexico after her divorce
to her parents just over the Border.
Then she got her bachelor's and master's
to teach French and Spanish at the college.
At a party, some curious friends
asked how we met.
"I heard her cries from the Rio Grande
so I leapt in and saved her."
All heads turned to her.
"So I saved him right back," she said.
They liked that; all sympathies swung to her.

My wife's hair now is no longer dark
but white like an erotic angel.
Her eyes have the wet light of morning grass
suggesting life has been uneven.
At night she sleeps next to me,
touching me with her own thin lines,
her own thin hands, except in the summer

are shadowed by light silks
as she lies across the bed gentle and open.
Ah, to have someone so to sleep with!

I had her painted in oils, something permanent.
Someone has to be the last love.
At the end in the hospital
she whispered to me, '*La vida es sueño.*'
And, it was.

Dating Le Professeur de Français

Merci, merci I never knew such intimacy
could be found on the college faculty
for she's become my joie de vie
in every instance never a pièce de résistance
for that's the best part: sleeping as one
until dawn comes and night is done.

Chérie, don't you see, my lovely French refugee,
we live a vie sans ennui!
We were young and you taught me
to love with your foreign tongue.
I remember a dream once where you fell en Seine
so I leapt down the ladder to save you again
furthering international intercourse, of course.

Sometimes she calls me a 'cunning linguist'
repartee is hard to resist,
though liking cashews she never eschews the fat
while chomping more than her share of foie gras
without dropping any tidbits into her French bra,

itself concerned with stopping any outbursts,
even my French tongue has improved from
voulez-vous couchez avec moi, to je t'aime, chérie;
she taught me and I learned, you see.

She pretended innocence when I admired her blouse,
remarking she had admirable je ne c'est quoi,
but I let no double entendre turn our amour asunder
better to suffer from déjà vu (wouldn't you?).

I asked her to marry me and she said 'oui',
since a raison d'être makes things better, you see,
though I'm still all agog, afraid
she might leave me for some frog.

Call Me Ishmael

We sail on the morrow for alien oceans,
so on our last night we all came ashore
except the Cap'n who just watches the sea alone.
'A single moment can quickly become all'
quoth the dark Queequeg, quaffing his rum ration
by unbending his body into a stark rising curve.

'We create continuation of things we've lost',
adds the Chaplain trying to keep
everyone on a long table of memory,
'while their resonance will haunt us
making us different from what we were.'

He said on the sea is a stillness of things
where waters there float on forever.
Here on land we have our hard, sure places,
but the sea stretches always on
until it rejoins itself, for
the truths about time and space
must be many with unending oceans
running forever all around us.

We could see Ahab still on the prow
dark in the late sun, looking out to sea,
as if trying to look beyond it.

The insights sobered us; as well,
this lanky, raw primitive had surprised us,
with both men suggesting a profundity.
The voyage should prove interesting.

The Good Old Days

The early Hindus came closest
to the truth of life,
writ in ancient Sanskrit
that everything was finally one
and each was actually all
as everyone has lived other lives.

I remember best being the tiger,
slipping about unseen
as one with the jungle,
striped like reeds and bamboo,
mating with sunlight, or the moon at night,
sliding smoothly as the grass moves.
Then meat muscle slam down
wrench neck snap dead
teeth crack cartilage
red taste wet food.

Later a fierce coupling of blood passions,
a coitus of fang and claw

where we felt fully for the moment
two become one.
I really did like that.

The world was easier to understand then.
Does nobody else remember?

Alzheimer's and Senescence

Around my old neck hangs a heavy chain with an
imprinted disk holding name and home phone
as I use my Alzheimer's aid more, for not
remembering means another hollow place, another
nothing where I remember something yet I get
into confusion so my wife says the disk gets me
back to the people that care to find out who and
where I am and feel whole again as I never knew it
was so easy to lose things since it's best not to
think if you want sleep and when I refind a few
things comes a rush of memory enough to feel real
again in myself that is existing as a muddled mind
center old and gray and out of control whose main
job is keeping track of my glasses for there is little
more anymore as a man is only his own past
which can't know he's not so I put on the disk to
remind myself nothing's changed yet sometimes I
remember more but can't remember why so I try to
look inside this shadow world knowing things
only get worse not only with who I am but sex

demands different attention for sometimes we still
feel around and are more alive and less alone when
we hold another and for a short time I think I am a
real person with a body that will feel things until it
doesn't while we live by reaction and turn around
the suspicion we're shadows of something else
which must be our own memory though at times
I don't know myself for many realities live
inside and hang on as things get lost and have to
get used to being alive though my head empties out
and I fear a long time alone while everything
gets further away and maybe the end is empty.

Visiting the Cemetery

We want our memories to live on their own
like a red balloon on easy-sloping
hills of summer-green grass.

This image never goes all the way away
though we avoid the chiseled stones about
where the dead writhe and rustle
like rats scurrying in the earth,
tunneling like the Viet Cong underground.
Maybe the dead do whisper among themselves.

Sometimes our universe seems to shift a bit
in some lazy refrain of slow-falling rain:
nonsensical recalls, perhaps,
but everything has its own truths.

Mona Lily

No mere a portrait would do;
I wanted a painting of Lily.
Her eyes brown, so brown,
sure and still, not nervous.
A trace, perhaps, of some old sadness
so easily finds her face perhaps.
Evening shadows shift, about slightly
as the softness, the stillness,
create a sense of grace.
We don't often get to see the world so,
rearranging itself around us.
Lily becomes real at once:
no self-conscious portrait poser
but someone with a memory
of things being broken,
someone who has come back
better from a sad before.
Do we read too much
into even Mona Lisa's half smile?
Sometimes there is so much to sort out

as memories must mix in
to this smiling woman with sad eyes
wanting no more surprises.
It is fine to be loved and safe.
She knows I want her to feel this way.
I know myself that black wall well
my first wife died years ago;
I was the ghost left behind.
Many of us have our own hollow places.
With the last light fast fading
come a slight smile and sad eyes
glistening like dew in dawn grass.
Illusion always lies inside the image:
ah yes, my Mona Lily.

Maybe One More Life

After seventeen years his ex-wife wrote him
a long letter saying her second husband had died.
She wondered how he was,
suggesting maybe they could help
with each other's ghosts.

He hoped nothing would happen before Saturday,
then he would find out what she really wanted,
and make damn sure she got it.
Life suddenly had a resonance
for never should he have ever let her leave.
Once eleven years ago when his sister died
she came alone to her funeral
to hold his hand, kiss him long on the cheek.

Life's slimmer near the end,
being alone reshapes so much.
In long nights the sounds of clocks
seem to know something
while the dead are quiet in their own grace.

He and she would touch each other again,
feeling a something in the dark
deeper than any animal awareness.
When we die we will wonder
if we know anything or nothing.

He will now mow the grass back,
letting the long lawn green up
all along the water the way she liked.

Ubi Sunt: A Sonnet

He dumped a bushel of gardenias on the bed
and let them become their sheets
while he felt around and found her
as rain on the window let them
create their own privacy and place.
Then they entered each other's bloom
and let themselves blossom.

In the last summer storms come old ghosts.
He would reflower her forever
but life always has a last time.
Autumn leaves, winter awaits;
he will keep her closer.
He whispered he'd been saving
the very best for last.

The Last Conquistador

The rumors were wrong;
we wanted too badly to believe:
the golden cities were but adobe and dry straw.
Weeks later beyond brushy fringes of stubble
were green watersigns of the great rainforest
letting light seep through a lattice of leaves
as soft fruits sweetened to high color
in vine-clogged confusion overgrown.
Greasy-feathered vultures hopped stiffly,
tearing at ragged fur in the brush.
The coastal peaks raked rain from snagged clouds
by ripping out their black underbellies.
We found mountains sloping right into the sea
so steep men climbed out of the surf on all fours.

Women with bare breasts like avocados
mated with us eagerly
in a musk of panther and ripe bananas.
Then some assumed a secure place:
those who slept with soldiers
did not have to carry supplies.

The locals led us that last day to the great sea.
Over the final ridge the earth fell away
into the Atlantic as the sun burst
at the end of its long curve
drowning, throwing its death throes
across a full sweep of sky and water, tilting
Byzantine sheets of bronze, slashes of gold
piled high in columns of cumulus.
We could feel the colors --
fierce reds, the full spectrum now burnished,
burning out the last blue.
Streaks of light flickered as seabirds dipped,
sharp slanting, acid-streaked etchings
interfacing with the ocean's immense mirror:
a giant wheel turned a last turning
as water-birds fled for shore,
some still out so far.
This New World was a place to die,
for it has forever in its unending sky,
there in the twisted sun; maybe
to be reborn anew in forms fresh, unremembering:
dying, falling, dying, and all was over.

We had a moment: a seam showed us a new world.

Last Day in Ward D

No longer can I keep track
of everyone in my white room.
Old ones are not at our best near the end,
dying when weakest, at our worst -
which, I guess, is fair enough:
it lets me know it's time to go.
I'm so tired of trying to see
one more dawn, one more day;
voices around get further away.

At the end so little is left.
Everyone around me tries
to hide the emptiness.
Medicine makes everything easier,
without event, with little feeling.
Where I'm going has no time at all.
Children think we'll get wings.
I want my wife and wings.

A Sonnet on Domestic Love

I've seen my wife like this before, afterwards
when she walks around like a stunned bird.
She once told me, 'Okay, Romeo,
we're not here for a rodeo.'
A blossom once, but a flower still,
she fans a faint dazed glow
since we all have our own seasons.
We are two old pairs of wrinkled pajamas
twisted all around each other,
not as much a passion anymore,
but just glad to be there,
knowing we are seeing
some of ourselves in the other,
so we would never let go.

The Old Lovers

We old ones are not unique to want
a place of pleasure over pain
for age means some sad hole lay behind
recalling engaging anarchies of sensual excess
climaxing in collapse of each into the other.
Now old flesh and thin hair are last pillows
for fusing that moment of two into one
for each is a moon dependent on a common sun.
When near sleeping we keep close track
of each other, not afraid of death at all
as it would come naturally merely
one lover easing into the other,
feeling all the years before
settling back into a welcome place,
for old lovers like young want that sense of one
where they can lie for awhile forever
until light as dawn comes around
finding one alone.

Romance, Memory and Metaphysics at End of Days

We all wonder sometimes about our starspaces
being, indeed, more than empty places,
showing little ardor or any purpose
in their cold forever dance bereft of desire.
We pretend a forever afterward
with slow music and soft fiddles,
a false somewhere with no there there,
another malady mislaid, I'm afraid, milady.

How life once changed when
she wrote she was waiting for me!
It seemed something was working,
as we lay about each other again
seeking that subtle ding-an-sich.
She put herself in my empty heart
and kept things from falling apart.

Metaphysician, Heal Thyself

Well, I had a wife and a life;
after all, it's the personal that's important.
Subjectivity is feeling for the truth, too.
My wife gets upset when I try
to figure things out but what else
is finally worth doing?
It's important to know what you don't know.
At least there's a clear place to start.
I don't like not knowing, nor being afraid.
Better to die attacking, but my wife has died.
Einstein established that energy and matter
are ultimately the same.
Nowadays the new String Theory is staggering
stating the universe is not near-empty at all
but filled with subatomic, charged strands
(and matter does really matter).
Encompassing energy channels
of dangling ganglia might make
an obvious basis for finding a dead wife,
may even mean all is a changing forever.

Maybe we were never meant to understand our world;
though possibly it's the main purpose:
perhaps the universe is not scattered sun/star systems
but a single overall entity in itself,
an encompassing oneness,
quite possibly with its own overall consciousness.
Whatever it is we are a part, yet apart.

Psychic Evolution

Signs of Life

Text within image: Mother Instructs Small son on Becoming a saint

Mother Instructs Small Son on Becoming a Saint

Breakfast at Padre

Alien Fruit

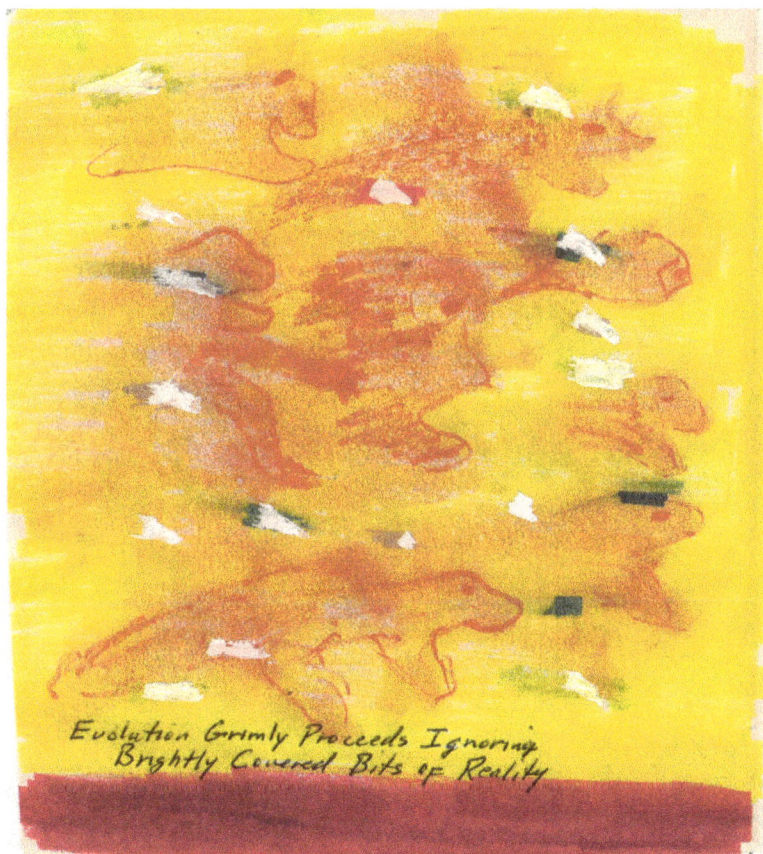

Evolution Grimly Proceeds Ignoring Brightly Covered Bits of Reality

Fish

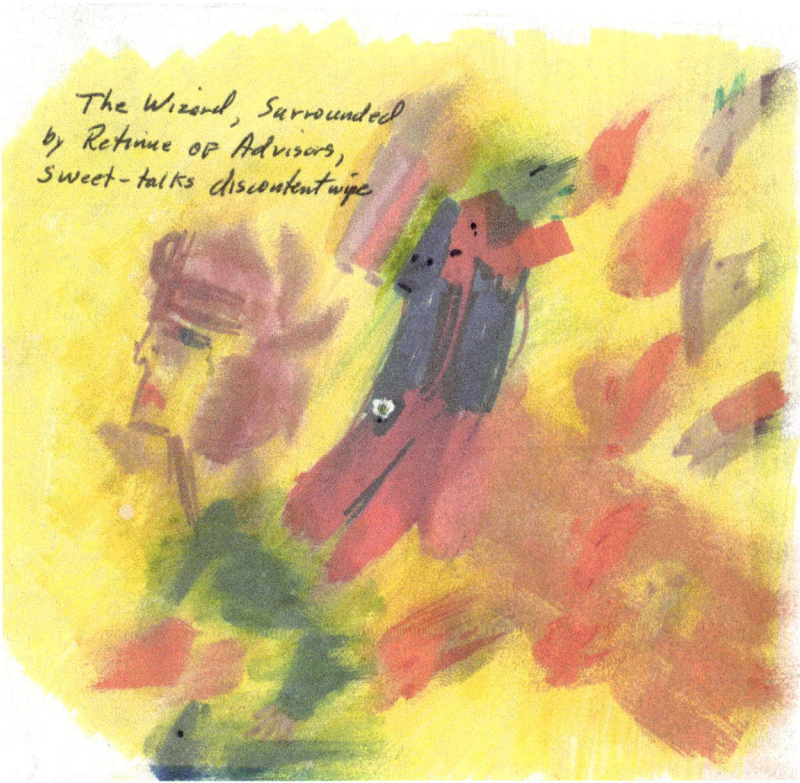

The Wizard, Surrounded by a Retinue of Advisors, Sweet-talks Discontented Wife

Universal Possibility

Wall with Window

A Sunny Day with Sex

Fish

 A Beautiful Woman Rejects the Absurd Notion she was Once a Fish

A Beautiful Woman Rejects the Absurd Idea She Was Once a Fish

Man Invents Himself

The Days Dwindle Down

We know when we're old
life is only a little longer,
'Don't worry,' she said before
we married so late in life,
meeting at a civic dance of some service club
in a huge auditorium with an orchestra
playing, but nobody dancing,
embarrassed and all sitting stiff.
She sat across from me,
so I asked her to dance. She leapt up
and we gave it a go in front of hundreds.

By the next number a full floor.
Back at the table she was the center
like any new heroine of yore.
We became each other's date then and there.
The next morning she came to my apartment
to make breakfast, bringing her own stuff.

Lovers in old age know
we love because nothing lasts.
Two months before she died

she surprised me, tears filling her eyes,
saying it was so good having a last love.
In the evening I go out into the backyard
trying not to let emptiness become all.
At the end you can't ever
let your last love go.

Love and Loss

On slow-passing, languorous nights
we listen to the tides riding over
slopes of sand with long
shallow fingers of sluggish surf
coming down and closer to us,
whispering what we can almost hear,
while knowing slow changes are near.

In the sweet anarchy of nighttime we touch,
hold each other against the darkness,
knowing one old lover will be left behind.
The tide teaches us its lesson,
with its earnestness so bittersweet,
for nothing stays, all goes away
letting invaluable old dreams disappear.
We will always lose everything,
though still we have to love what we lose
to make our memory stay.

We lay together on the night beach
with unknown space spreading to forever,
merely old lovers trying to stay within
easy reach of each other,
sensing the insistent stirrings of nature,
eager to feel them forever.

Bells Ringing in an Empty Sky

She's buried across the river
under high canopies of no-nonsense firs
as the sun warms the earth around.
Rains soak down to find her,
to help carboned molecules become new leaves
whose lifetime is to follow the sun.
Death takes so much with it.
In winter's monolith it is easier to see forever,
never to wonder why we were so excited
then, when we thought there was a way to be.
Now one lover wakes alone,
never to find the other forever.
Death takes so much.
Coming from the churchyard where she lies,
the bell tones hang long in the night.
A presence thins out softly
filling the empty sky with itself.
We can never know the real truth,
only feel it.

.

Depression Deep in the Outback

From Perth I followed the Swan River
already shallow, into the rainless endless Outback,
then farther in my four-wheeler
trailing a scent of petrol,
tracking the dry traces and dawn sun
to the empty middle of a map
which shows only immense paper lakes
with dotted shorelines, in reality
mere salt plains waiting
for the hundred-year flood
when some immense Pacific cyclone
can punch inland this far
to fill a shallow sea.
Only once did I see any sign
of man: a low wooden cross
where some outsider emptied out.
For sure it was not an abo,
not a protoman who knew
his way around on any walkabout.
Nature's patience exceeds our own;

that is the truth in these great, long silences
stretched between monolithic chords of a slow fugue
laid ever-eternal in unhurried sequence.

I scanned the alluvial sidebanks
seeking first for gold, later opals in the heavy clays,
mining underground during the day
to come out in the evening, exhausted,
into a cooler, beaten-down bush,
to revive a consciousness worn so thin.
I have lived my whole life waking
from stupors, then slumbering again.
I see myself as a shadow -- a mere memory of myself
sleeping under a white-bark Australian gum
that grows only along those ghost waterways,
those dry washes always waiting for rain.

A few men have gathered here.
Each lives underground where it is cooler
and works his own claim. At night we come up
to feel the temperature drop fifty degrees.
The stars are fixed and firm, hard and constant
in a sky ever without clouds.

I took a minerals course at the community college;
my wife was not pleased. She never suspected

this was not about us at all
though her lips tasted like winter wines
and I stroked her hair at night.
Now I am alone and she is alone,
now only shadow seeing shadows.
The empty land feels full of ghosts.
Our own terrible star staring so close
looking me eye to eye on the salt pan
will burn off all shadows, leaving
a bleached skull stuck on a stick.

Sometimes hard women in AC campers came out
to service the miners for exorbitant sums,
making him remember his once-wife;
so much was sealed away long ago,
here where never and ever are the same.
This nothingness makes it easier
to forget something that once was
for we exist in what is, even though
the secrets were sealed so long ago
letting a long silence linger.

There's too much nothing
in this land of no colors
so far from the sea.
Yet in this flat, blanched hardscrabble

lie great beds of ancient mollusk shells
abandoned by the ocean millennia ago,
now waiting out this long arid season
for one reality to again evict another.
I came here to be where everything is open,
but found that everything is just empty.

All final secrets are insidious, enseamed inside
the air we breathe; the cruel bone-sered clay
caches shiny metals and precious stones
below its brutal expression, bereft of love.
Perhaps this great silence itself is the truth:
a last illusion left.

The Alzheimer Guy

People with Alzheimer's disease knew before being
told but people don't know how it is to forget. Recent
history is first. It goes away little by little, like
where you live and how to get there, anything past
or planned. Walking on a sidewalk may end on a
wood's path. Memory is like having money in the
bank though you will never get to spend it.
The past is gone. Often I remember an image
but can't put anything with it. I remember that once
I could remember. On everyday topics
like the weather I'm okay and can talk easily.
People are interested and it's easy if I make a few
jokes. It relaxes everyone if they can laugh and kid
around a bit as I do. Sometimes I tell someone I
know all his secrets but don't worry because I can't
remember them. I remind them then they can use
the same jokes again though probably do that
anyway. I carry around my name, address, and
phone number. Never have I forgot my name but

I told my wife that the other info comes in handy. I
write this page all at one time, or I'd forget what's
written and have to start all over. You got to use
what you got until someday you'll forget you are.
Nobody wants to be here and not know it. In the
mornings my wife sometimes asks me who she is so
I still know and say so, making a small joke like
'well, you were my wife yesterday.' She likes that
and things get normal and I'm glad I had
enough sense to marry her. I know that the
other me is not the me now, but at least I still know
that I was. Soon nothing will be in my head because
I'm not dying but disappearing for I forget to be.
Maybe it will be better not to remember what I was.

The Old Lovers Live in the Present

My first wife died decades ago.
I love the former, love the latter:
they always seemed the heart of the matter.
There is no other way to be.
It is a slow spring day today,
watching things that never stay,
that wait their time before going away.
Again someday an old ceiling fan
will turn slowly overhead whispering
"She's gone. She's gone. She's gone."

The night slides by beyond time,
because all is subjective without excuse
in a reality neither never nor forever.
While outside weather rustles the window,
the world takes a timeout in the early a.m.
Holding my hand tight, my wife
says I lead a rich fantasy life.

There's not a lot of time left, I'm afraid.
Tonight we'll lie in bed together remembering,
letting the river of time overrun us.
We stay lovers even as old-timers,
though nothing need ever be hurried,
which is fine since we're where we want to be.
In the mornings we are all about each other
and every night Achilles is rewelcomed abed.

A Man and A Woman

(For Lilly)

In the whisper of a silken swish, she undresses:
the static of a peignoir sliding on smooth skin.
Lilly in her late fifties is young to me.
In a late Indian summer
she's a flower opening
in an easy nonchalance, relaxed,
confident inside the moment,
She would be upset if I left afterwards.
But I did not come to leave.
We open easily, each to the other.
My hand moves over her silks.
Her eyes go soft and see just me.
I could lose myself here,
not as animals just joining bodies
but a man and a woman closing
each unto the other.
I ask if she wants me to stay over.
'Yes', she says, 'over and over.'
Soon, we will probably say the words

for life's empty spaces now seem too long
to let such a woman go, you know?
We are the older ones
so society leaves us alone.
I will hold her close
here at the end of the world.

Play It Again, Sam

My wife died fifteen years ago and it's still not
okay though most of life is little choice while
long and uneven but now for the first time I can
feel the last time and even the end of my own
life although once we could touch each other's
hair and at the end I felt the brittle bones in her
face like the boats moored in our bay on a thin
line their long lights winking on and off in the
sea's slight shrug before she said she'd like
to die while it rained making it more intimate
in our memory, an image that would stay close
in our heads so we would be sure to remember
the other in the next reality and reconnect even
by instinct for who knows how those things really
work though maybe the final answers will be
too simple to be true even though time and
expanding space and even infinity now hide the
real secrets so well that early Hindus suspected
identity is illusion as nothing was ever fixed
apart in the first place though simple things settle

like the day's light for play before sun goes away
and eventually no lamps need be lit because
it's all us anyway as I hear the quiet but feel the
darkness and she once said that's why we're
here, but could have added 'being together'.

Winter Wine

We may be old but our skin's not cold.
This old poet lying with his unclothed wife
finds her still so much more than
a Cook's Tour of the way things were.
I readily admit having a lover,
making our small world an occasional ecstasy
(though her coffee is grounds for divorce).
Even if our advanced ages sadden the season
with raw mortality edging into reason,
our bodies feel each other
for a feast, a fest, finally
even a fait accompli.

All I really know of existence is gleaned
from Ptolemy and column B.
But surely not all will end well:
no more she, no more me.
In the mornings I hold her,
my hand on her shoulder
while our enemies grow older.

With women you can spread yourself shallow,
or run deep with just one and age with her
for there is no resonance in an empty wineglass,
while winds fill in our handprints on each other.
The end won't be easy with so much to lose.

Christ At Qumrun

The long lines of the land are unchanging,
ever blanched and ever barren,
showing no color and expecting none
as seen by the desert-dry Essene eye.
A single hawk hangs in an ash-white empty sky
this land is larger than any life, where less
is more; even our presence is an act of will.
We are here to reflect Him and live his ways
making this place pure and pious.
Dead Sea waves flop greasy
on black mud in this rainless waste of land.
Stone, sun, wind, sand:
just the basic elements for truths have hard edges.
The goats find little food.
Without real rain or any sweetwater,
papyrus and date palms suck life near deep drawn wells.
Hyenas, sliding obscenely on their bellies
nose into the night troughs, run away
with loose mouths full of offal.
We drink sour goat's milk,

finger hard dates in a gritty pouch.
We observe many days of fast.
Baked bread is all hard crust, dry grains
ground to powder then wetted to paste.
Romans ignore quiet Qumrun,
move about only in columns
so zealots can't pick off stragglers.
Their foot soldiers huddle in Jerusalem.
Nobody wants their thin copper coins
stamped with false gods, nor
their war eagle mounted on our shamed Temple.
Soldiers put hands inside the women's folds,
feel their unclean flesh. We live
away from women unclean in sloughed blood
who ride unwashed, thighs muscled
from the camels that spit at us.
Rome has no power here. This is
God's province; we, His people
make our own Temple here,
keep sacred rules written,
rally the village families for the coming Kingdom.
So near: the Messiah is coming.
The Spirit will cleanse us as the desert is scoured.
He who baptized me, John the Baptist
who is one of us, has been murdered,
uneasy is this foretold time of The Promised One;

already hundreds claim to be such.
Staged miracles and false messiahs are all about,
preaching old truths with new words.
Out of the sand and salt of the Dead Sea
from a purity scoured clean:
where the right ways have been kept,
the Messiah must come, from here,
where we're gathered to keep the true heart alive.
Christ is the Holy Spirit in a man.
God is the Father; we are his Christs.
I, too, am said to be such.
The old temple is corrupted
only we Essenes have kept things holy.
So the elders want to send me out,
saying they see the One in me.
We here are all sons of God,
all lambs of God to be sacrificed and red-ripped.
I am such a Son.
We live the laws we carefully copy.
Our only choice is to face God;
after that there is no choice.
The skies will peel back and the world will be
not as we know it but as it truly is.
That which changes knows not, for
living men can know nothing;
only the Holy Spirit can know the truth,

but I must bring hope so all may know
they are special and have a home in Heaven,
a home in His heart.
As the Messiah I will promise them that
we prevailed in Egypt and will also with Rome.
If these days remain corrupted
Rome and history will use us as their own
and no one will know who we were.
We leave these scrolls buried in dry caves
near the Great Salt Sea
perhaps for eons beyond our own
for a judgment not ours to give.

Old Lovers Grow Older

With perhaps an overburden of experience
we did marry later in life;
falling so easy into each other surprised us
but it seemed simply the place to be.

We still argue some, but stay close
as lovers do, for to lose the other
would be to lose my life.
Nothing is ever forever, though
when younger we got around pretty well
but found since a better way to be
by having someone to be afraid with
whom we can hold all night.

She was the one I picked.
She says I was smarter then,
but with a resistance to common sense.
She dutifully wrote her memoir
while wearing her worn peignoir,
letting instinct prompt older mates

to sleep even closer to each other, for
where young lovers once touched,
old ones want to revisit.

A bell rings in an empty sky
reminding us we love because we die.
If she dies first someone must show me
where I can find her, where we'll be together
and matter no longer matters.

An Importance of Being Ernest

The Serengeti is a simple world, primal,
as is stalking the black-maned lions
in the Ngorongoro Crater near Kilimanjaro.
The sex is strong and straightforward.
Some places, Paris too, make life important.
With a woman you're either in or you're out.
Fair enough, for things need to be simple.
Women and war give men a way to be.
Liquor, slow-sipped, lets feelings resonate,
lets life make its own connections.
One has to hold to his own code
to be sure his life stays his own,
even the ending of it.
One always has to be ready to die.
Someday his body will betray him
when memory no longer remembers
the women, the writing, the wars,
the wildebeests on the Serengeti,
and how he learned to love them all.
Death is one's own devil to deal with.

A Haikuist's Life of Good Years

my lovely wife waits
wearing nothing under her
woolen winter robe

the moon surprised us
lying next to each other
never to untwine

silky long loose hair
brushed looser for her lover
to spill over his loins

follow the seasons
to the end for you will find
your love waits again

The Poet and His Wife as Old Lovers

Her flesh is soft and lightly scented,
in its own organic way even subtle,
so we touch, not letting rhetoric run rampant,
allowing the libido its own way.
With scented loins and soft eyes
she created her own fuss all around us.
Once on vacation we loved
in our aura of the blue Aegean,
lulled by the bliss of a calm, accepting sea.
Someday soon we will have a last place to lay
letting memory gently fade with the day.
We live in the moment,
even pretending sometimes a soft
sadness doesn't underlay all.
At this point my wife threw my pencil away
before I had a chance to yell 'ole'.

Visiting My Wife on Her Birthday

Shade is so deep grass too green,
tombstones are way too many:
I like being here but dread it too
for she comes closer, though never to touch,
just to let me know yet again
that once she was and we were.
I look about, embarrassed
that I may have loved
her more now than then
though I have to take what I deserve.
It's also her birthday today
and I have no present
just peace.
My new wife says I've learned
quite a valuable lesson.

The Loop of Loss and Beginning

He lost a wife: she, a sister.
He could not be consoled,
for her it was easier:
she had to save him:
the trick is to stay busy,
keep the feet going
until it passes, until it passes,
towards numbness, away from feeling.

They saw parts of many movies
ate often without appetite,
observing long rituals of food;
she started smoking again.
Market lists were made
for drives to distant stores.
Evenings were the worst:
a temptation to touch the pain,
to see it was not some mistake.

Tonight he cries during the news;
their faces trap the tears between--
tastes of salt, tastes of each other.
Mouths, lips touch; lips press
for contact beneath the grief,
for the whole joy of relief.
She hoped this would happen,
though was afraid it would:
she feels his hand come over her
straight for the heart.

Siva Returns

Ever older than Earth,
I tore shards from ancient stars,
created whole universes, filling in
long centuries of silent nights.

I was reborn yet again
in this volcano, not the awful isolation
most imagine but one forged by fire,
a seed of seething terrible feeling,
an uneven birth of stretched granite
mounded in a huge horn, thrusting
black, butting the red sky.

Growling gut-deep I fused elementals, fundamentals
by stirring fierce fevers and old, old needs:
flushing hot fluids, loosing carbon by fire
forming primal proteins and strings of fruited ganglia,
my chaos creating life.

I spewed wild-blown ashen flowers that filled a world,
forming acid soils for soft green jungles,

searing, cleansing the too-comfortable countryside
and recasting all the easy curves:
new forms for old: I really did like that.

Crusted over now, cooled into a fixed form, I still
overrun the green edges of human hedgerows,
threatening anarchy and stoking deepest dread
as stiff-feathered dark hawks ride downdrafts
to sweep smooth over the rough-ridged diversions
marking free-running unstoppable slides to the sea.

At the fringes of my huge crater fidget
timid foreigners and distracted tourists –
those builders of structures so easily crushed –
peer uneasily into Earth's horrible hollows,
curious about what's down there, what will come up?
Kids want cokes while wives worry about restrooms;
the men feel the warm fresh-firmed slopes,
look for little lava stone souvenirs.

The illusion of separation soothes humans
unaware of my ever-changing nature,
of faint blood-screams from deep broken bowels
and slow evolutionary alleys.
All will see me again someday.

The Old Anti-Semantic Poet Invokes Anarchy

Well, I feel that things are
quite bereft with little left
with nothing new now coming
and all else gone away
with only pontifical phrasings in play
swiftly outshining the sun's last day
as lyric balloons soar high and away
at stanza's end, relieved
of any jest or zest.

Thus we say our last goodbyes
like word balloons in Miró skies
in friendly fluff-filled stanzas
without any real rain or pain
to find ourselves finally
in cloudy prose-filled forevers
allowing all that'd left to stay
well-satisfied in the quiet lust of light.

The old poet lay with his wife,
each so easy with the other,
knowing there are times
to make things just-so,
others to let things go.

Love Among the Ruins

Shared passion often slips into intimacy
making older age more interesting
with new nests of meaning.
But will memories live longer than lives?

Once she was lean and loose-limbed
sprawling about their bed
as they lay loosely in each other's layers.
Now her hair is so thin;
he can feel bone under the skin.

Physical love is more than mere touching
more than an assault with a friendly weapon.
Now he was too old to do it well:
so was she. Still, they did it,
sharing old sins and old skins.
He puts his hands gently on her,
there where DNA imprints have made holy places.
For life's a thin winter when the leaves have left.

They touch each other again:
maybe exists a place of grace,
maybe of meeting, of merger,
where memories outlast lives,
where sea and sky seal without seam.

A Red Balloon in an Empty Sky: Images of Miró

Picasso's Cubism had ruptured the rules already
so the art world found other windows
using data, even from Dada, seeming relevant,
that imagines in its own language of images,
sensual yes, but a new artistic view.
As Miró's white clouds swarm overhead,
seeming up and away far from the fray,
free to roam just as they wished,
awash in winds of whim.
Anarchy invites a freedom of free-flowing forms
liquid and evolving, finding
a way to give old realities new license.
We see like kids lying on the lawn
just watching those fine Miró clouds float by,
for painting was his poetry, figures unnatural
and every portrayal meticulously arational
in a surreal overlap of terrestrial and celestial.
How nice to live away in a Miró day
with swollen clouds shifting and changing
and a lone balloon almost-alive

holds its red in all that blue
while the plains below are green forever,
and the day is most stuff
of triangular children, colored-in of course,
in simple solid colors of a world within itself.
This balloon is away from all pain
and all is reborn again:
a child at play is serious stuff,
though when boots and trucks come
the tiny Miró triangles are mashed in red,
those human shapes with eyes like ours
in a war where love is short and pain is long.
Everything lies broken apart.
Then the world got better as it sometimes does
and Miró kept evolving, and change is good
as children delight and critics gape
at his simple love of color and shape.

The River, As Ever

The moon makes the late shadows longer,
the stars seem too far away to be real.
She watches the dirt road from the river,
knowing no other way to stay his wife.

Her father owned many rice paddies
and was, as well, a wealthy merchant.
As children they were ever together, playing.
Once he took her rice cake
she started crying, so he came back,
sat with her and cried too.
During the summer rice festivals
the village had its own long table for the families;
the two sat always together talking and laughing.
When she came of marriage age
her father immediately offered a decent dowry;
his father accepted at once with no negotiations.
The village was stunned: such was not the custom.

Seven years ago the Army came in a big boat
to take all young men for the war in the North.
Faint rumors from faraway were never good,
so every day she watched the road to the river.
She would know his walk in an instant.
He never came back, never any message.
Still she watches all day until the loss of light
when ghosts of the moon wobble on black water.

The morning river mist drifts through the trees
where they played as children.
They would have had their own child by now.
Bright flowers in a short season.
Skies fill with the rush of rain.
She lets herself listen.

A Farmer in the Fields of Forever

A thin haze hangs in the early morning
before the breeze carries the brace
of open pinesmoke, here
where the wilds have been cleared,
though along the river the thick trees are safe.
Grasses keep trying to fill in the footpaths
that follow natural curves of the rolling land.
Crops in their seasons come and go
while the old forest waits to fill in the fields.
Limbs are cut and stacked
as winter is again waited out
with a thin smell of firewood burning all about.
As always, our dusks are another's dawn.
Farmers die finally;
then they and the land seem freed
each from the other, though
their bodies will break down
as they, too, become the land:
dying as we all die,
even emperors and old poets.

The Year's Last Haikus

I. Spring

ah April again
bird eats first butterfly
I waited for this

II. Summer

alone on the lawn
I learn I can paint the clouds
any color I want

III. Fall

I am but can't be
such is the center of things
where we will not go

IV. Winter

in the winter snow
I touch the cold back branches
my wife is so sick

A Walk with Walt

I would love to learn from you
and would walk and talk,
with you if you go my way,
if not, we will always talk another time
for nothing ever goes away,
just as nothing will ever stay.
Sadness and happiness are finally the same
for we all feel all things
at once without letting life be separate
and anything lost comes around again
so we will welcome it back and wonder
where it has been and what it has seen
for finally one finds he is everything.
I choose to talk and ramble as I wish,
for it is all me and mine and all I must do
is include everything into my life
so I will see I am one with it, for
we are, all of us, made of the same stuff.
I will stop for awhile if you wish to reply.
I will either love or listen, for you are me also.

If you are in my way then move aside
or show me why I must stop.
For I wait for no one, though I
would talk with Emily for hours if I could.
Like Krishna, I too roam all about
not rhyming much, just staying in rhythm
with the moon and the tides and lovers.
While I am here the world is mine though
you, of course, feel the same way.
Come, let us walk the land,
if you wish to stay it would
be fine; we will again be together.
For I would always be one with you,
even in the early a.m.
We are each the other, and the other is us.

The Seasoned Lovers

'Ah, old lust and last love.'
She smiled when I said it,
laughed whenever we did it.
such a woman so gracious, so bodacious,
a radical ion to really keep your eye on.

A woman wishes for you to find her
but wants to see you searching first.
In some metaphor of one to three
she was definitely more,
for I never met a four before.
She laughed, liking that accolade.
Often I watched her workout,
arms making hard circles in the air.
Early on she debated between
being prude or nude. Thank God
she chose the latter, ending the matter.

As young lovers we each caressed the other;
as old ones we just hold on
finding ourselves hanging, swinging in time
at the end of all weakening line.
Some day all will just go away.
Life's like a momentary smile;
it's only here for awhile.

Ubi Sunt Les Fleurs

He dumped a bushel of gardenias on the bed
and they became their sheets
while he felt around and found her lips
and all his favorite private places
as rain on the window let them
create their own privacy and place.
They entered each other's bloom and blossomed.
In the last summer storms come old ghosts.
He would reflower her forever
but life always has a last time.
Autumn leaves, winter awaits;
he will keep her closer. He whispered
he'd been saving the best for last.

Not Much More Time

When I visit her in the hospital
we recreate our trips sailing
in the balmy Indian Ocean
to the South China Sea, sleeping together
on layers and layers of blue and orange silks
with the sun sliding over a far end of the Earth,
pulling fierce red sunsets away.

Now I can tell her of another voyage
to an Antarctica of huge blue icebergs
all floating solid and serene,
holding the sun frozen inside.

Wars End Slowly: A True Story

Hidden away in green mountains
a string of backbays lie off Leyte:
Japanese zeroes, out of bombs,
no longer strafing, came in as kamikazes
looking to crash into our warships.
Heavy guns close by almost broke his ears.
But a Jap plane found his destroyer.
My dad's best friend, Luke, blew up.
They found him mangled on the steel deck.
One leg lay in a red slaughterhouse
swamp of gore and tissue,
connected by a lone blood vessel.
Dad picked up the loose leg, pushed it
next to Luke's body on the stretcher,
then ran back to his gun station,
hoping it was still there.

In the nursing home solarium, decades later
the Navy awarded Admiral Taylor a medal.
He stood in his hospital gown, a bit confused,

finally saying ' he'd forgotten why he was here
but that it sure beat the alternative.'
The audience, relieved, loved the line.
His last day ended on a good note.

At his service, my new wife met Dr. Luke Abel,
now a Houston heart surgeon famed
for helping develop the artificial human heart.
Luke walked well, though with a heavy cane.
My wife remarked what a fine man he was;
so I told her the true story of Leyte.

Ms. Lily's Last Lover

We talk softly before sleep;
later when I hold her we're even
more aware life is running out,
knowing often someday someone won't wake
as we await the ennui of eternity.
Even scarier is an enemy we can't see,
letting old age feel like a fragment
of life floating in clouds of chance or chaos.
At night I easily find her
loose hand looking for mine in the sheets.
We let our fingers touch the other's
with a real perseverance insisting
loss is never fated even though
each feels a lover growing ever older,
yet still hoping words
and feeling can find forever,
as late summers remember snow,
as lives fade away like thin pencil lines.
Sometimes after letting libidos run rampant,
'stirring the senses' as they say,

we trust old lovers to find their own way,
afterwards to slumber, holding one another
with no sorrow or tomorrow sure to follow,
wondering if we must leave
our bodies behind like fallen leaves
to be buried in separate places.

Going Down

The stewardess strode briskly down the aisle
saying to return to our seats
and something about the tray tables
in a voice a little too excited.
Then the captain came on the intercom
saying 'circumstances were adverse'
as the engines were down so we couldn't circle
but had to come straight on in with cabin lights off.
The stew told us to fasten seatbelts
and put all seats in the upright position.
The young couple in the seat just ahead
shifted about jerkily clutching with frightened sounds
as our plane dropped out of the sky.
We said love and goodbye.

Finally we heard the engines kick in,
moments later a violent bump on first contact
before the tires started squealing, then cheering
as we sped fast but smooth on the runway.
The captain didn't have to tell us

that we were finally okay, but he did.
A roar again as the jets reversed to slow down.
The cabin lights went back on;
everything looked quite usual.
An old couple in the back still held hands.

Afterward, my wife admitted
she had been glad we were old, though
on the way home she said maybe
the couple in front had the right idea too.
Always we remember saying love and goodbye
while the plane fell through the sky.

A Brief Précis of American Poetry

Walt, who made himself the American Krishna,

becoming larger than life to see it all;

Emily, whose cries for hope were never answered

by someone to talk to or read what she wrote;

Ezra, whose clean, clear Chinese images

became finally a muddled psyche in poses;

Thomas E., who made his own impotence everyone else's

by scattering all the puzzle pieces;

Wallace, who lived an upholstered life

Examining things as they are while amused by the irony of existence;

Also thousands of self-conscious MFA's who push Pushcarts of well-typed poems

so carefully sensitive in their streams-of-consciousness;

And I, who deserve neither destiny nor sour grapes,

since I had the stupidity to start at seventy.

Where the Old Poets Go

Do you think an old scribbler who once published
with the likes of Jose Luis Borges and Ted Hughes
doesn't know that what he once was
he isn't anymore, that
he now lives in the land of liverspot and forgot?

There is something to be said
in favor of living fast before dying in a fire,
or even fleeing from an estranged husband,
for the only thing left to behold,
to write about, is being old.
You have to stay with where you are
since it's simply so, merging
what you knew with what you know,
letting the spirit sink poignantly low,
burning itself out with embers of insight
a long invite, maybe forever but so slow,

remembering what once you were, wondering
why the new words won't come anymore.

So be it! You write about finding
where you are for you know what you were.
Life's wonder was easy in its own energy,
now you have to write of loss,
trying to make death mean something.
The rhythm and tone of things
was always more important
than their impertinent melody.

Ongoing Negotiations Between Animals, Us, and Reality

We hide our dread inside the Earth
layered already with feathered shells,
lumpens of leathered skin and matted fur
sealing the smells, and eyes emptied,
no longer caring about the coming of spring.
Blame a tired poet with a lost, dead wife,
remorse, bad lungs, and little insurance,
coughing up grey clots and wondering
will he ever walk again in the woods?
An indifferent moon bobs on black water.
I don't want to die but will have to take my turn
as long lightyears sing their own song.
Since empty space needs no one's permission
just stack the dead in meadows, letting
flowers bloom in white-washed bones.
Hard edges do have their day
prodding us to purposes not always our own.
For we want to mate on perfumed lawns
with lush women dripping from the sea

who caress salty bodies and bones,
feeling faint pulsings of soft tissue
as matter seems to matter, even so
logic leads only to a old dead owl.
The sun keeps steady, reassuring and restirring
those perennial red herrings of the particular those
wonky kookaburras, yellow cats stalking
chalky cormorants, shoaled salmon in rainbow array
as such a mélange of menageries ebb and flow
while tides come and go from the sentient sea.
If cosmos and self are really the same,
then apparent disorder is order unnamed.
Perspective, as ever, is all.

Dawn ghosts never want to go away
and poke me awake into an unreal ether
with no thin hand to hold beneath the covers.
I try to find my way through feeling
to celebrate a plain sense of things.
The air itself becomes very heavy
as motion slows and sounds stop
while an ineffable sadness fills all spaces.
Sometimes final truth seems less important
and I don't want to go alone
for we are animals ourselves,
and at least we are home.

Requiem for the Poet

He said life was short though seemed so long
as all his art had become chaotic;
also, he refused to rhyme anything,
said it made his head ring.
After a man in a van said 'amen' yet again
the undertaker did quickly disperse,
unfortunately the drinks were on the hearse.
Having died before his time,
for he found life less than sublime.

The body was laid in an empty grove.
Nothing alive was left for he was boxed-up
so animals couldn't munch lunch,
so no matter. Nothing
was said, nothing was read,
not even one of his poems.
They buried his books with him
to be his only comfort,
though the bindings will break and deteriorate
for paper's organic also.

His wife and girlfriend both left behind,
thus the sullen group was quite subdued,
for nothing was festive, the mourners restive,
fiddling with cell phones and pocket computers.
Little was read, little was said:
it was cold and he was dead.
A wake followed with bottled water
and sour grapes surly served.

Unfortunately there was no way home
for the pre-paid package
did not include a return trip.
 (He would have wanted it this way).
All he left anyone was this poem.

Ah, Ezra

Ezra Pound could be simplicity itself.
The images were all. If he remembered
'A group of girls on the beach, and
all were kind of pretty but one
who was fat, and the boys were throwing
sand on all the pretty girls', the poem
would end only with 'the fat girl moving over
to get sand thrown on her, too.' That's all.
He let the image alone say itself.
If you explain a feeling, it is none.
Poetry seemed new when so much depended
on Williams' red wheelbarrow glazed with rain.

Pound had extraordinary language skills:
enough to translate Ancient Chinese and find
Li Po and his lessers had left their lines for him,
creating spare and strong images
that evoke only a single emotion:
a woman waits years by the river for her husband;
a bereaved man hears not his dead wife

on the walkway but only winter leaves;
A man celebrates because his house burned,
enhancing his view of the mountains.

T.S. Eliot's stack of images was a treasure trove.
Ezra threw out more than half, leaving
a selected sprawl to represent a fragmented world.
"The Wasteland" noted him as 'il meglior fabbro'.
What the poem is, is what it means:
isolated images in a disconnected world.
The poem fit well the times;
to scholars it became an endlessly engaging puzzle.

Everything has to eventually fail.
Ezra's wits became muddled, his manner confused:
in World War II he broadcast anti-Semitic tirades,
at surrender was imprisoned for war crimes
as old literary friends rallied 'round.

Soon his melange of languages, including
Old Greek and Sanskrit, made little sense.
His unending cantos were no longer coherent.
Treated benignly, he was finally released,
a bit befuddled yet surrounded by friends.
He still lived, still ranted, still tried to work:
poetry-wise once, now Pound foolish,

sinking in his own Sargasso Sea.
He listened to evening storms filling with rain
until America's enigmatic poet was gone.
Ah, Ezra.

The Older Lovers

Old lovers often seem just half-awake,
often sleeping close to each other
as if trying to remember
who they once were.
The nights last longer now
but that's not all bad, for
we find the other a fine place to be.
My wife is the best looking
grandma in a peignoir I ever saw.
We are mates, and interaction has slowed:
but that sure beats the alternative.
Feeling each other breathe,
we find our existence quite shared
as arms and legs wander about
always from here to there,
ending up almost anywhere.
In a dim past she was once my mistress;
we still touch in an early-morning bed,
always so easy with the other,
knowing as we are and as we were,

living lovers still existing, each
always in the arms of the other
for love has its own license
knowing always everything ends.

An Old Poet's Last Poem

The job of the poet is to make words alive
achieving an awareness in sound and meaning
while staying within a stream of consciousness
and moving in catchy whims of curious whimsy
flesh can be supple and even subtle,
though sensuality does wonder and wander
often ending up quite frayed, I'm afraid.

He knows when he's gone too far
to ever consider coming back,
ignoring all pleas to please
keep the poetry polite, the stanzas slight
and don't try pushing light into night:
just so at the last it's eggnog for everyone
(a scribbler can create anything he wants
merely by making his narrator a madman).

A prose poem is most amenable
to a buffet of beauty thrashing about
(truly a pro's prose apropos Ero's pose).

Maybe my wife's stray limbs wander my way
so I endeavor to wind them in.
In our dark bed I can feel her fuzzy head
so I hold her softly foreverafter;
we old ones stay happy in our way,
as we worry for yet another day.

My Wife Went Away

My wife's pain went somewhere else
though she still liked me to touch her,
but only her lungs moved with machine help.
I pressed her hand with mine
so if she felt anything
she would know she wasn't alone.
I always hoped she would squeeze back
but she never did, she never could.
Once her eyes did seem to see me,
but her hands were cold.
I don't want her to be alone in there.
Sometimes she stirs in her sleep
at images, perhaps, of something else,
as we hold onto each other
in an otherwise empty night.
All of us live an existence that can't be,
so maybe there's another
where soft curves of flesh press together,
each reassuring the other.
Inside me something stays alone

but she'll always be gone
and I will always know it
in a slow life full of soft memories
still alive, though all still seems only a dream.
In death we simply sleep unending,
each never to meet again?
Perhaps we never find each other,
like living forever in an empty house.

The Alzheimer Guy Sees Himself

The light moves in and out of memories
and all I can do is stand here
trying to think what to do
then someone comes by and stops
asking me if I'm lost so I show him
the card around my neck with a phone number
and he stands with me until
a familiar car comes up
and a woman inside who is real nice
who says don't worry she's my wife
and everyone's happy I was smart
with my card which I put back on
so I felt good I did a smart thing
for I remember being a kid once
but maybe we get smarter growing up
though little by little I'm getting lost.

Life with My Wife on the River

Herons glide all about
without moving still wings,
large turtles bask on beached timber
with alligators no more, though
they still live further south
as the river softens,
slowing near the sea.
At night the moon rides the current
seeming a living thing, wrinkling,
then stretching its glints of gold,
borrowed pieces of the moon
which steals them from the sun.
We'll stay as long as we can.
That's all we can do.
I'm an old guy losing a wife,
too worn to welcome another life.
She is failing; I see the end,
but not the nothing beyond it.
We have to love what we lose
to make anything worthwhile.
We have to love what we lost.

Where is the thunder god whose
rabid wrenchings crack the heavens?
It never seems to rain anymore;
the world remains without water.

Black clouds scud over a high moon,
stirrings and shiftings all about.
I want skies to spasm, ramp up in pain
and rain and rain wetting the world again,
sluicing and soothing its secret ways,
rustling like animals in the undergrowth
as the black river carries a broken moon.

Her skin was red in a late sun,
her hair black on the pillow;
low in the sky, so who could lose
a wife that came in colors?
But touch stays a long time,
especially if we listen to the rain,
living on my own on the edge of alone.

Endless World

I watch farmers forever folding open the earth
in long rows that go ever on and on until lost
at last in the long curve of the Earth,
running always away from us.

Only sad songs can be sung
in lifetimes too short for encores.
No one else lives here now, but me.
My wife's ashes are in the ground,
still at home in this green place, always growing.
I like this sense of her being here still,
for life is a place where so much gets lost.

Memories never ask permission, for
I need to be further away before looking back.
Better to find a final sense of things.
I walk back over the old byways
where once-worn paths are grown over with weeds.
We are on the edge of some meaning, some flow,
moving so slow to even know.

Just bury my body near the river with my wife:
my bones and flesh will dissolve in the dirt
for the roots to find and feed on.
I will be meadow grasses and great oaks,
their leaves forever following the sun.
Let life become more open,
as I stretch out and out and out.
I am an old man empty and existing,
angry, yet still in absolute awe of it all:
worlds without end. Amen.

Dry Thoughts in a Dry Season

The doctor said the cancer had come back.
Now I wait it out in my own bedroom,
a small world of custards and cream sodas,
to rest and find a reason to die.
Crutches become clumsy in small spaces
so I crawl on hands and knees to the bath
to press close on the cold hard tiles.
A bedpan waits in the corner.
My wife lives now in the guest room.
With everything gone, how will I know who I am?

Sleep only settles during daylight.
At night I just at watch out the window
as the sea wind comes up and huge oaks roll,
big canopies blowing wild, free spirits stirring,
a rushing of life unloved and love not known,
sweeping dust and ash all the way
to the far Caymans and even Cameroon
where green overgrown green in endless orgy.
I merely guard impotently against silent enemies

slipping around shadowed corners
hugging the dark house, looking to enter.
No horsemen now this old country
of dried-out desire and dead friends.

But in my room a thin metallic whine
whistles in the air grilles.
A stiff brown leaf crumbles in my bed
leaving dried bits in the white sheet.

Master of the Romance Languages

I asked her once what she thought it would be
for one of us to love the other?
'We will see,' she said. 'We'll see.'
That was way back when the darkness
was kinder to a late hour habitué.
In fact, late night maneuvers
helped win my wife's heart;
a French teacher herself,
she fell not for entreaties
(voulez-vous couchez avec moi)
but by my being an engaging agent provocateur
with key maneuvers in the late post meridian
where carpe diem becomes carpe femme.
We often go there again.

A Head's up on Halloween

We old ones are really grey ghosts
in an anarchy only answerable to ourselves.
So beware, though things are not bad, for
the old eat the young only on Halloween.

Yes, young America, the old are going to get you.
They slide about in the shadows, at the edges
where children often play.
Have you not seen them in the darkening dusk.
Watching for juicy ones to wander off alone?
See the hunger in our empty eyes;
the children are our just desserts.

Come to our dimly-lit homes for 'trick or treat';
but look for that mouth-watery grin without chin.
Come to us on a quiet street,
for we have the tricks, you are the treat.
We have truly a special, quiet place
where you will be the object of grace.

Guiltless myself, I have done my job macabre.
But be comforted, for the good die young.
Thus do we return Halloween
to a Druid day of the dead.

A Walk in Winter

Thin gauzy clouds drift high in pale blue
wavering between being and not being.
When the fresh fields were open for seed,
as a young man he could never see
which woman loved him the most,
letting the best ones leave and be lost,
until he first saw his wife gathering hay.
Many of the maidens were as pretty
but she was smart and smiled.

He wanted her so much, she
with skin golden in summer,
even fiery in late sunlight
like the pond at sunset where
the ducks were black on red water.
His wife-to-be also came in colors.

But she died way too soon, so soon,
leaving without even a real goodbye, letting
the world become an empty room in winter.

One cannot live without some sadness:
the price for coming here is leaving.
The small cemetery nearby is green and quiet,
graves full of old bones in their best clothes
waiting for those they love to lie with them.
Maybe the dead do talk among themselves.

The sunset at day's end:
a small death suggesting another.
He had followed his seasons to the end;
if nothing is ever forever lost,
maybe she waited for him,
warm under her winter robe.
On his last night he would fall
so easy off the end of the Earth.
Loss is memory of happiness:
a feeling from real things.
As always a sad walk it was.

Lingering a Moment Longer

A poem in the evening, just one,
like a woman or glass of red wine
with its taste of French summer coming
as expected, the second week in June,
early enough to blend the tannins
with the sugars, since resonance is all,
letting life linger
and making moments longer
before all moments are no more.

Carpe Diem Indeed

Years ago I found a place where
dark colors split a violent sky
with a new woman who was
in herself another whole world,
but where we rule it's for a short time
as things went away in ashes and dismay.

Years later she surprised me
like a lone, lost bird in an empty sky,
this presence from one who had echoed forever,
with a story of sad, unending days
from somewhere a long, long way away
saying she was available again.
Even old idiots know enough not to say no.

I will keep self-implied promise
with no carping, no tedium, no carpe diem -
to seize the day, indeed; *carpe femme*, I say.
We shall gather our rosebuds along the way.

A spring rose budding, a May bud rising:
no mere image in a poem for thee,
no rhetoric of memory for me,
no pretense of fleshy immortality.
At the end we'll be together still,
together still until all is still.

Boy Meets Girl

The overlap of lust and love
has always attracted our attention,
Striking at the very core of intention
to ask the diva on the divan to dive in,
a vital compound of sagacious and audacious,
an invitation only Prufock could refuse.

From then on its all downtown
with lots to work out all around,
like the first discomfiture of a new easy chair.
Then all´s safe at least until
you find out what you´ve found.
Life's long gray day has nowhere to go,
and the present has no place to stay,
so we play and wed and die anyway.

Boy Met Girl

Once I found a place where
dark colors split a violent sky
with a new woman who was
in herself a whole world
as her energy became my own,
but things went away in ashes and dismay.

Years later she surprised me
like a lone, lost bird in an empty sky,
a presence once echoing forever,
with a story of sad, unending days
from somewhere a long, long way away
saying she was available again.

Even old idiots know
enough not to say 'no'
for life is loose and open-ended
and it would be fine to find it again.

Love and sex easily overlap
but are nevertheless not the same thing,
though their infusion has romantic
and quite pleasant confusion.

Just a Little Lust in the Dust

There is no way things are supposed to be;
so we simply go the easiest way
as scientists claim in Darwin's name that the species
evolve a consciousness to care for themselves.
So remember when one's own mate
was a fresh flower to see and touch.
That's when this poet became an amiable, rambling sort
letting languorous, sensual, magic sentences
meander on and on and on,
not letting life become
a humdrum, human, conundrum
always needing a beautiful sweet sonnet on it,
like waking his perky wife to see
sparkling dew diamonds on the lawn.

All's Better with a Blues Sonnet on It

I bemoan the absence of absinthe
as my wife slights my absence of sense
with brain lost in idle reminiscence
which to her means mere senescence;
perhaps things begin and end in i
especially if no one will ever pay us.
('Too much tumult,' said the janitor
in his odd rambling iambic pentameter.)
So I suggest we all flee this ennui and see
what there really is to you and me,
putting both raw and sublime into real time
as I'm glad to have my say
well before all goes away today
for all's better with a blues sonnet overlay.

A Muse and a Full Wind

My poems start well enough:
an opening idea, a single incisive image
to be developed with appropriate detail,
maybe a control metaphor about mankind
moving finally to a quick couplet to close
with a sudden shift to subtle irony
(well, so far so good).

Life is long but too short.
Something happens after thin images
start to stir on their own,
spinning off shards of metaphysics and madness.
The sonnet simply cannot hold,
and anarchy is loosed among the muses
ruining resolution and even reason itself.

Primal discovery does run very deep
though all things must connect
beneath our pale salted seas
where poets are Ishmaels all.

Worlds Without End

One morning I stirred but she didn't.
I reached over. Her body felt different:
her heat was gone. I touched her face;
she wasn't there anymore,
Only a shell seemed left behind.

We poets often pretend everything doesn't end,
that all will be together again
as long rows ever go on until lost.
At last in the long curve of the universe,
only sad songs can be sung
in lifetimes too short for encores.

My wife's ashes are in the ground,
at home in this green place always growing.
I like this sense of her being here still,
on the edge of some meaning,
some flow, moving too slow to ever know.
Just bury my body near the river with my wife
as bones and flesh dissolve in the dirt

for the roots to find and feed on.
I will be meadow grasses and great oaks
with leaves forever following the sun.

Life can't be but is.
So everything must be somewhere.
She said he'd find her.
I am an old man empty and existing,
angry, yet still in absolute awe of it all:
these worlds with end without end. Amen.

Table of Contents

www.ingramcontent.com/pod-product-compliance
Lightning Source LLC
Chambersburg PA
CBHW060744100426
42813CB00032B/3395/J